BOOK

OF

DEATH

生死，人生歷程的始末

培根／奧修／愛倫坡―― 等人合著

王凌緯―― 譯

目次

編序	生死，當所有巧合成為絕響	4
I.	塵埃已落定	8
II.	暗夜中無所遁形	46
III.	通往死寂的單程票	98
IV.	精神綠洲	160
V.	置之死地，而後生	224

編序
生死，當所有巧合成為絕響

　　一天的開始，始於睜開眼睛好好呼吸。隨後手提著公事包，踩著皮鞋搭上人滿為患的大眾載具，將自己調整成面對生活的最適狀態，積極而正向，讓所有黯淡的可能都轉化為生存動力。

　　與乘客們一起移動，車窗外景物飛快地過了場，留在車廂空間的只剩對生活璀璨的遐想。然而你在這充滿朝氣的一幕中，隱約感受到唯美虛幻的背後，正有團黑霧悄然直上——你看見下班後的夜間車廂，昏黃下只有無精打采的幾個人，全無生氣。回神過來，站在這明朗無瑕的地方，只消閉起雙眼就一片漆黑。列車還沒進站，而途中有什麼被遺漏了嗎？

　　舉凡人間，無事不遵循既有的法則路徑，但這樣一來似乎太多禁忌。快樂與傷悲，抑或天堂與墓園，你很難不發現兩者為共生，而並非因果。自然而然，

若不在伸手不見五指的黑夜裡，肉眼根本看不見星光；若非殘破和死灰散落四周，心底也不會妄想復燃。

　　死亡，是自古以來的恐懼；停止心跳、呼吸曾經和雷電一樣令人費解。它彷彿將一無形物從肉體抽出，轉瞬之間，生命只剩下軀殼，空氣也逐漸失溫。有人說，那被抽離之物便是靈魂——可想而知，最早的信仰總與死亡脫不了關係，重生或是復活的希望全寄託在神話之上。不過，人雖自古害怕死亡，但長生不死也無可否認地使人生畏；由於不死而成為妖魔的傳說，世界上無所不在。

　　曾試圖追求永生的人，也都成為了過客，幻想終究付諸流水。秦始皇多次派人尋找靈藥，漢武帝也網羅天下方術之士，不惜耗費巨量資源、時間來追尋長生。或許在某種意義上，他們是最「接近」長生不死的人物。尋思，若他們得道不死，在所有摯愛之物都離自身而去的今日，是否真能如願以償？依附著信仰，生命的意義也發生了轉化，延續自己的方式不僅僅是仙藥，而逐漸有跡可循。正如偉大的牛頓說自己之所以看得更遠，是因為「站在巨人的肩膀上」，但巨人們已死，軀體早湮滅在塵土空氣之中，卻還像是活生生、直挺挺地與後人一同望向

遠方，完整了永生的可能。他們靈魂的一部分已然融入社會、文化，抑或流竄在血管，潛移默化地架構出各自的意識，就像隻死不透的小蠱——誰又能在一隻微不足道的螞蟻身上，瞧見蟻窩的邊界和形狀？

面對如此不可違抗、無常的命運，從沒人能稱自己「真正死過」。對於活著的人來說，理解「生」的唯一方法固然是「生」，而理解「死」的唯一方法也只能是「生」——這是人們在通往未知的旅程上，為自己打開的一扇窗。

時間那條筆直的軌道上，車廂內滿載旅客。

也許彼此熟識或陌生，但各自都將在未來的某站離開。每逢有人臨走之時，便會在其他人腦海烙下這一幕，成為他此生的留念與寫照——《生死，人生歷程的始末》一書收集了數十位名家存在過的證明，他們也曾搭上車，彼此穿梭於不同時空，在列車留言板寫下這一百二十餘則生死觀察，最後全無例外，都到了站。

首章〈塵埃已落定〉是人生歷程的基調——生命之始出於無，凡是落入這場修行的靈魂，必先將這萬象盡收眼底，然後明白落葉終歸於根，生命隨時可能化作塵土。但死亡一步步向你逼近的事實，卻

讓人不願妥協，〈暗夜中無所遁形〉述說一種古老的恐懼，將你帶往煙塵瀰漫之地，被懷疑與不滿團團包圍；三章〈通往死寂的單程票〉描繪了「生」的收場方式，當到達了「死」那片萬籟俱寂的沙漠，意義這時才萌生。此時生者試著理出頭緒，為追尋一小塊樂土啟程，〈精神綠洲〉一章即是藉由內省而逐步理解生命的過程，待沉澱好思緒，路途也不再顛簸。

終章〈置之死地，而後生〉則有如雨後冒出的新芽，這小小希望既脆弱又強韌。歷經了恐慌與幻滅，生者面對這大千世界將脫胎換骨，懂得如何開始生活。

開往未知的途中，也許曾歷經黑暗與光明、炙熱與寒冷，卻終歸於平靜。你凝視遠方的地平線，一切都如過片般呼嘯而過。幻想著，若是站在外頭的某一點，望向移動中的車廂究竟是何種感覺？

你看見旅客們有說有笑的剪影，驚覺無論從哪個時空看往這裡，也都宛如著眼張張底片，只依稀看得見定格的節節車廂。緊接著發現，雖然死亡的地平線依舊不著邊際，但在這段生命歷程中的每個當下，確實都是獨一無二的造化，全部光影、聲音和感動也都是絕無僅有──眼下，所有一切儼然穿越了死的境地，而後義無反顧地繼續前進。

I
塵埃已落定

We are but dust and shadow.

——**Horace** 65-8 BC : *The Odes of Horace*

生死，人生歷程的始末

吾人不過是塵土與陰影。

——**羅馬詩人賀拉斯**《頌詩》

Death must be so beautiful. To lie in the soft brown earth, with the grasses waving above one's head, and listen to silence. To have no yesterday, and no tomorrow. To forget time, to forgive life, to be at peace.

——**Oscar Wilde** 1854-1900 : *The Canterville Ghost*

生死，人生歷程的始末

死亡一定很美。躺在鬆軟的棕土中，頭上青草搖曳，耳中充斥緘靜。沒有昨日，沒有明天。忘卻時間，寬恕此生，長保安息。

―― 王爾德《坎特維家的鬼魂》

生死，人生歷程的始末

BOOK OF DEATH

For what is it to die but to stand naked in the wind and to melt into the sun?
And when the earth shall claim your limbs, then shall you truly dance.

——**Kahlil Gibran** 1883-1931 : *The Prophet*

生死,人生歷程的始末

若不是裸身站在風中,消融在陽光裡,死亡還能是什麼呢?

當土地終於奪去你的肢體,這時你才真正開始起舞。

——紀伯倫《先知》

Dying was nothing and he had no picture of it nor fear of it in his mind. But living was a field of grain blowing in the wind on the side of a hill. Living was a hawk in the sky. Living was an earthen jar of water in the dust of the threshing with the grain flailed out and the chaff blowing. Living was a horse between your legs and a carbine under one leg and a hill and a valley and a stream with trees along it and the far side of the valley and the hills beyond.

——**Ernest Hemingway** 1899-1961 : *For Whom the Bell Tolls*

死亡不算什麼，他對死毫無概念，心中也無所畏懼。但生存就是一片坡地上經受風吹的麥田。生存就是空中的鷹。生存就是那只打穀揚塵中的盛水陶瓶，精穀盡出，秕糠迸飛。生存就是你胯間的馬與你腿下的卡賓槍與一丘一谷與林木夾擁的激流與谷壑的遠側及彼方的丘陵。

—— 海明威《戰地鐘聲》

人生天地之間，若白駒之過隙，忽然而已。注然勃然，莫不出焉；油然寥然，莫不入焉。已化而生，又化而死。生物哀之，人類悲之。解其天韜，墮其天帙。紛乎宛乎，魂魄將往，乃身從之。乃大歸乎！

人活在天地間，就像白馬飛馳掠過牆間小孔，不過是一剎那罷了。蓬勃之間，一切都出生了；昏蒙之間，一切都死去了。既由變化而出生，又由變化而死去，生物為此哀傷，人為此悲痛。擺脫自然的框架，丟棄自然的拘束，移轉變遷，魂魄要離開時，身體也跟著走了，這就是回歸大本啊！

——莊子 c. 368-279 BC：《知北遊》

I have seen a thousand graves opened, and always perceived that whatever was gone, the teeth and hair remained of those who had died with them. Is not this odd? They go the very first things in youth and yet last the longest in the dust.

——**Lord Byron** 1788-1824 : *Letter to Mr. Murray*

生死，人生歷程的始末

我見過上千個敞開的墳塚，注意到不論什麼消失了，逝者的頭髮跟牙齒都仍如下葬時完整。這不是很奇怪嗎？它們是年少時最早出現的，在塵土中卻又最為耐久。

——拜倫，致出版商友人書信

Each day is a little life; every waking and rising a little birth; every fresh morning a little youth; every going to rest and sleep a little dearth.

——**Arthur Schopenhauer** 1788-1860 : *Counsels and Maxims*

生死,人生歷程的始末

每一天都是整段人生的縮影；每次甦醒與起身都是一小段出生；每個清新早晨都是一小段青春年華；每次休息與入睡都是一小段死去。

—— **叔本華**《雋語與箴言》

生死，人生歷程的始末

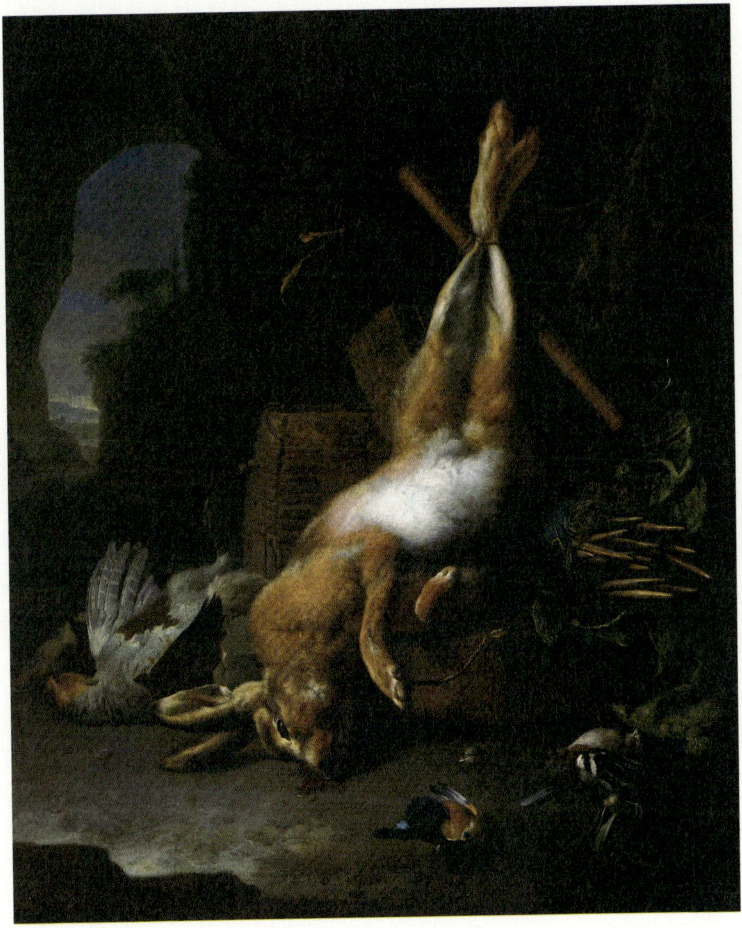

生也死之徒,死也生之始,孰知其紀!人之生,氣之聚也。聚則為生,散則為死。若死生為徒,吾又何患!故萬物一也。是其所美者為神奇,其所惡者為臭腐。臭腐復化為神奇,神奇復化為臭腐。故曰:「通天下一氣耳。」

生是死的同類，死是生的開始，誰知箇中道理呢！人的出生是氣的聚合，氣聚則生，氣散則亡。如果死與生是同類，那我有什麼好擔心的？所以萬物是一體的。人把欣賞的事物稱為神奇，將厭惡的稱為腐朽；腐朽能再化為神奇，而神奇會再化為腐朽。所以說：「整個天下是一氣通貫的。」

—— 莊子 c. 368-279 BC：《知北遊》

Death is a Dialogue between
The Spirit and the Dust

——**Emily Dickinson** 1830-1886 : *'Death is a Dialogue'*

生死，人生歷程的始末

死亡是一段
精神與塵土間的對話

──艾蜜莉・狄金生〈死亡是一段對話〉

Death is for many of us the gate of hell; but we are inside on the way out, not outside on the way in.

——George Bernard Shaw 1856-1950 : *A Treatise on Parents and Children*

生死,人生歷程的始末

對我們許多人而言,死亡是地獄之門;只不過我們是在地獄裡等著走出去,而非在外頭等著進來。

—— **蕭伯納**《親子教養大全》

On no subject are our ideas more warped and pitiable than on death...Let children walk with nature, let them see the beautiful blendings and communions of death and life, their joyous inseparable unity, as taught in woods and meadows, plains and mountains and streams of our blessed star, and they will learn that death is stingless indeed, and as beautiful as life, and that the grave has no victory, for it never fights.

—— **John Muir** 1838-1914 : *A Thousand-Mile Walk to the Gulf*

沒有其他話題比死亡讓我們的思想更顯扭曲且可悲……讓孩子與自然同行，讓他們一覽死與生的綺麗混融與結合，及其歡暢的密不可分，就如同樹林與草原、平原與山稜，以及神聖星河的諄諄教誨，他們會學到，死亡其實並無螫刺，而且美麗一如生命，而墓塚並無勝利，因為鬥爭已不復存在。

——美國國家公園之父 約翰·繆爾《墨西哥灣千哩徒步行》

生死，人生歷程的始末

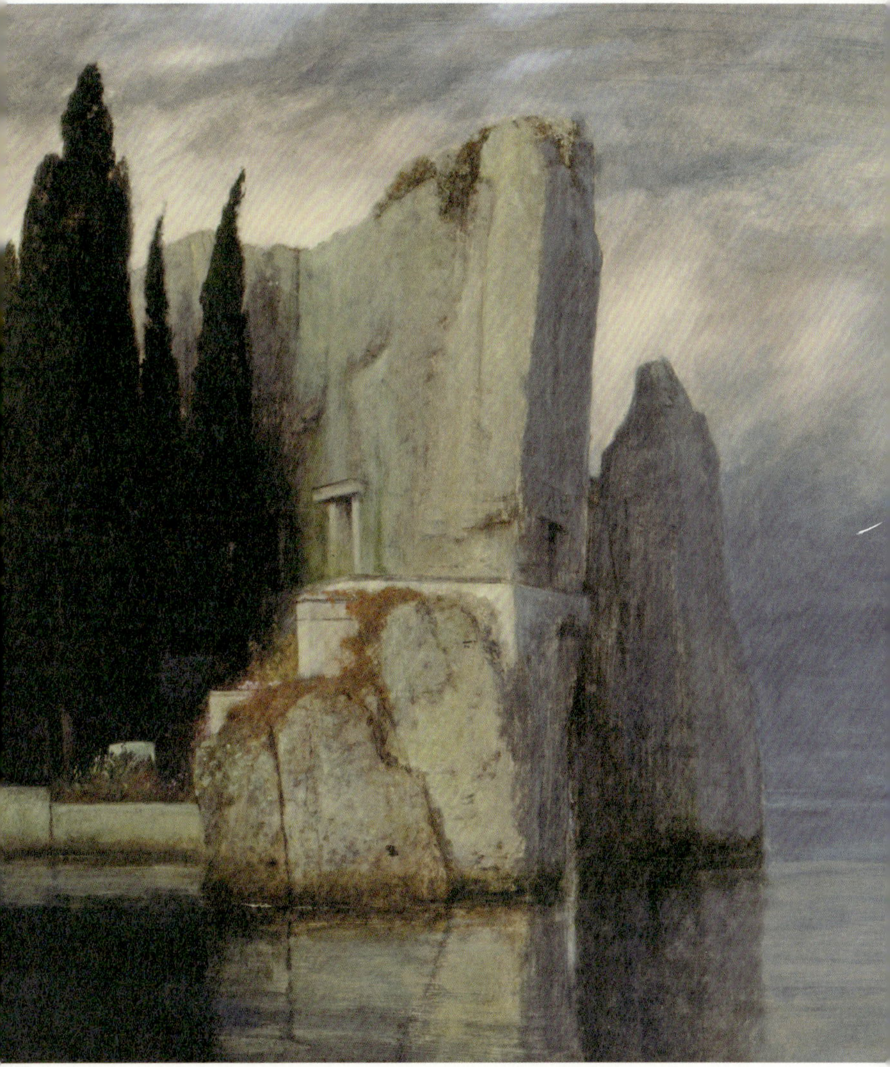

Sadness gives depth. Happiness gives height. Sadness gives roots. Happiness gives branches. Happiness is like a tree going into the sky, and sadness is like the roots going down into the womb of the earth. Both are needed, and the higher a tree goes, the deeper it goes, simultaneously. The bigger the tree, the bigger will be its roots. In fact, it is always in proportion. That's its balance.

——**Osho** 1931-1990 : *Everyday Osho: 365 Daily Meditations for the Here and Now*

憂傷帶來深度。快樂帶來高度。憂傷給我們根基。快樂給我們枝幹。快樂就像一棵伸向天空的樹，而憂傷就像深入大地子宮中的根。兩者皆為必須，而樹要長得越高，它的根同時要扎得越深。樹越高大，其根越深廣。事實上兩者總是成比例。這便是平衡。

―― 奧修《此時此地：奧修靜心 365 天》

The two most important days in your life are the day you are born and the day you find out why.

——Mark Twain 1835-1910

生死，人生歷程的始末

你人生中最重要的兩天,就是你出生的那日,以及你發現自己為何出生的那天。

—— 馬克·吐溫

He had no conscious knowledge of death, but like every animal of the Wild, he possessed the instinct of death. To him it stood as the greatest of hurts. It was the very essence of the unknown; it was the sum of the terrors of the unknown, the one culminating and unthinkable catastrophe that could happen to him, about which he knew nothing and about which he feared everything.

——**Jack London** 1876-1916 : *White Fang*

生死,人生歷程的始末

他對死亡毫無認知意識，但一如所有野生動物，他對死亡抱有一種本能直覺。對他來說，死代表最終極的痛苦。它是未知事物的真髓；它是未知的恐怖的總和，是可能發生在他身上最至極、且無法想像的災難，它關乎他一無所知之事，也關乎他所有懼怕之事。

—— 傑克・倫敦《白牙》

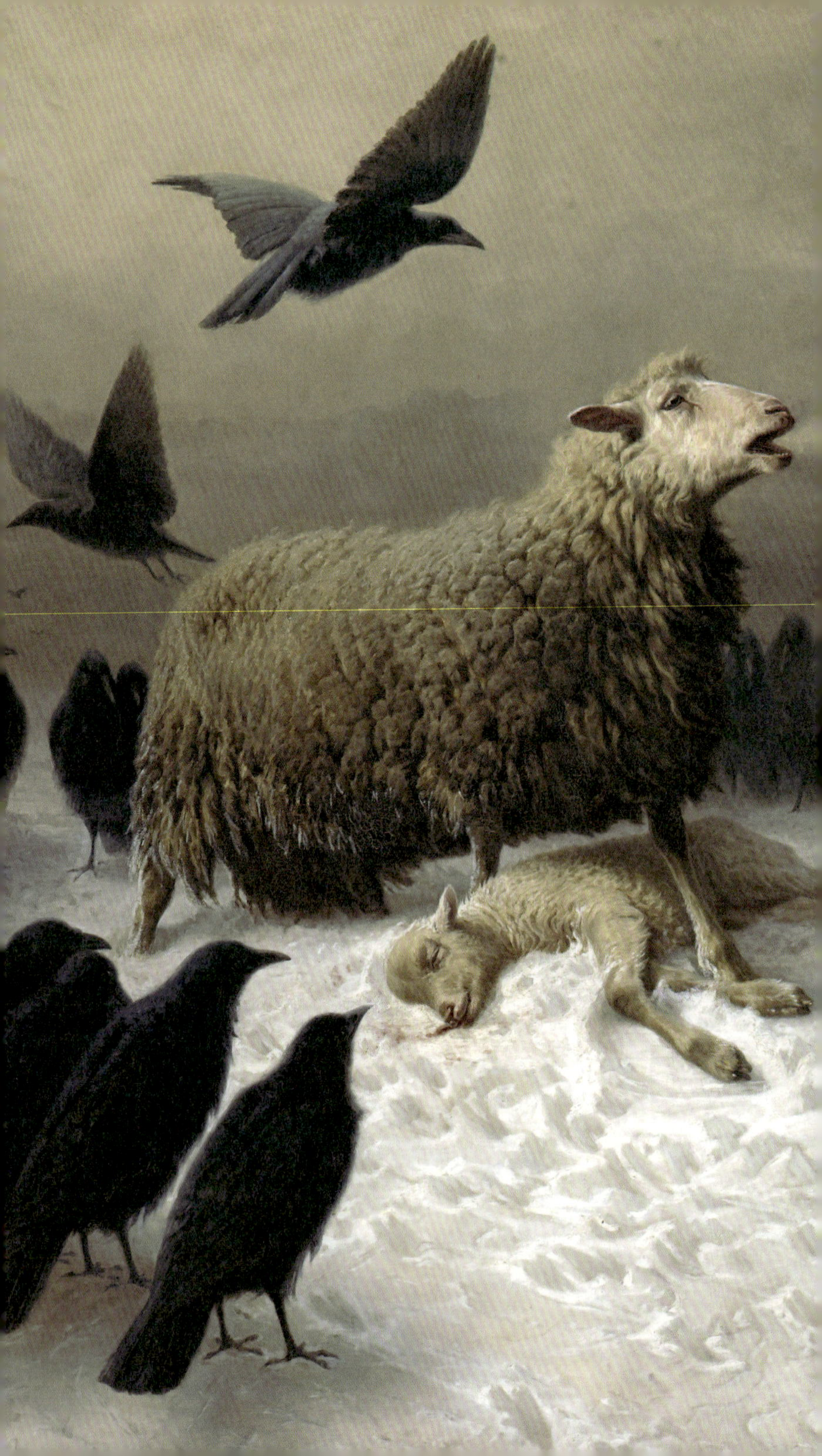

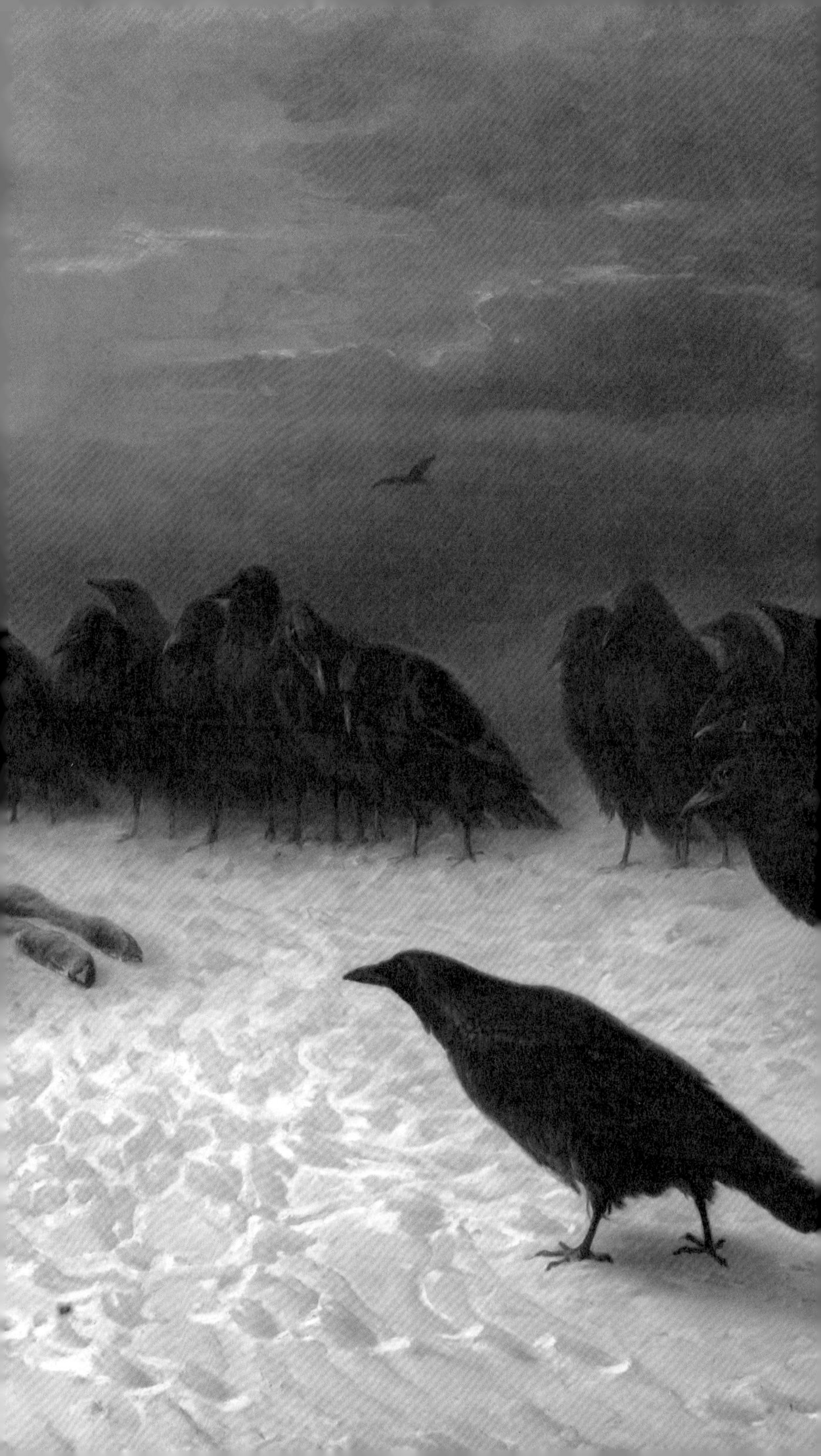

II
暗夜中無所遁形

Since the day of my birth, my death began its walk. It is walking toward me, without hurrying.

——**Jean Cocteau** 1889-1963 : *La Fin du Potomac*

生死,人生歷程的始末

從我出生的那天起，我的死期就邁出它的步伐。它步步向我走來，從容不迫。

——尚・考克多《波托馬克的盡頭》

Man cannot possess anything as long as he fears death. But to him who does not fear it, everything belongs. If there was no suffering, man would not know his limits, would not know himself.

——**Leo Tolstoy** 1828-1910 : *War and Peace*

生死，人生歷程的始末

人只要畏懼死亡,就無法擁有任何事物。但對死無所懼的人而言,所有一切都屬於他。人若無苦難,就不知自己的極限,也無法認識自己。

—— 托爾斯泰《戰爭與和平》

Death was far more certain than God.

——**Graham Greene** 1904-1991 : *The Quiet American*

生死，人生歷程的始末

死亡遠比上帝確實。

—— **葛林**《沉靜的美國人》

You've never seen death? Look in the mirror every day and you will see it like bees working in a glass hive.

———**Jean Cocteau** 1889-1963

生死，人生歷程的始末

你從未見過死亡?每天看向鏡中,你會見到它就像是一群在玻璃蜂巢裡幹活的蜜蜂。

──尚・考克多

生死，人生歷程的始末

· MORTALIA · FACTA · PERIBVNT ·

BOOK OF DEATH

I do not fear death. I had been dead for billions and billions of years before I was born, and had not suffered the slightest inconvenience from it.

——**Mark Twain** 1835-1910

我不怕死。我在出生前早已死過千千萬萬遍,並未因此蒙受絲毫不便。

—— 馬克・吐溫

Death, a cause of terror to the sinner, is a blessed moment for him who has walked in the right path.

——**James Joyce** 1882-1941 : *A Portrait of the Artist as a Young Man*

生死，人生歷程的始末

死,對罪人而言是恐懼的來源,對為人正道者卻是受祝福的一刻。

―― 喬伊斯《年輕藝術家的肖像》

You cannot find peace by avoiding life.

——**Michael Cunningham** 1952- : *The Hours*

生死,人生歷程的始末

你無法藉由逃避生命尋得平靜。

—— 麥可‧康寧漢《時時刻刻》

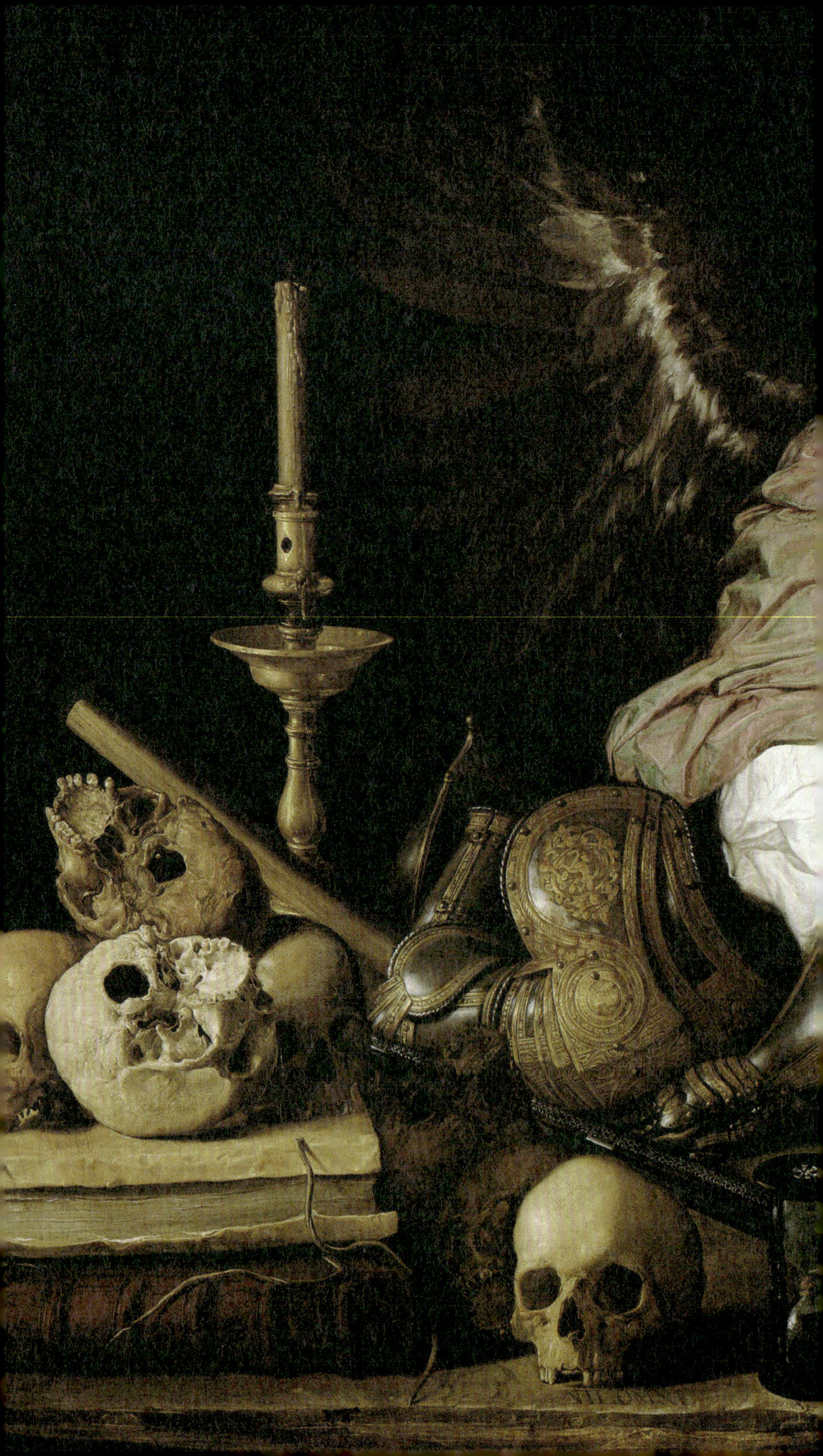

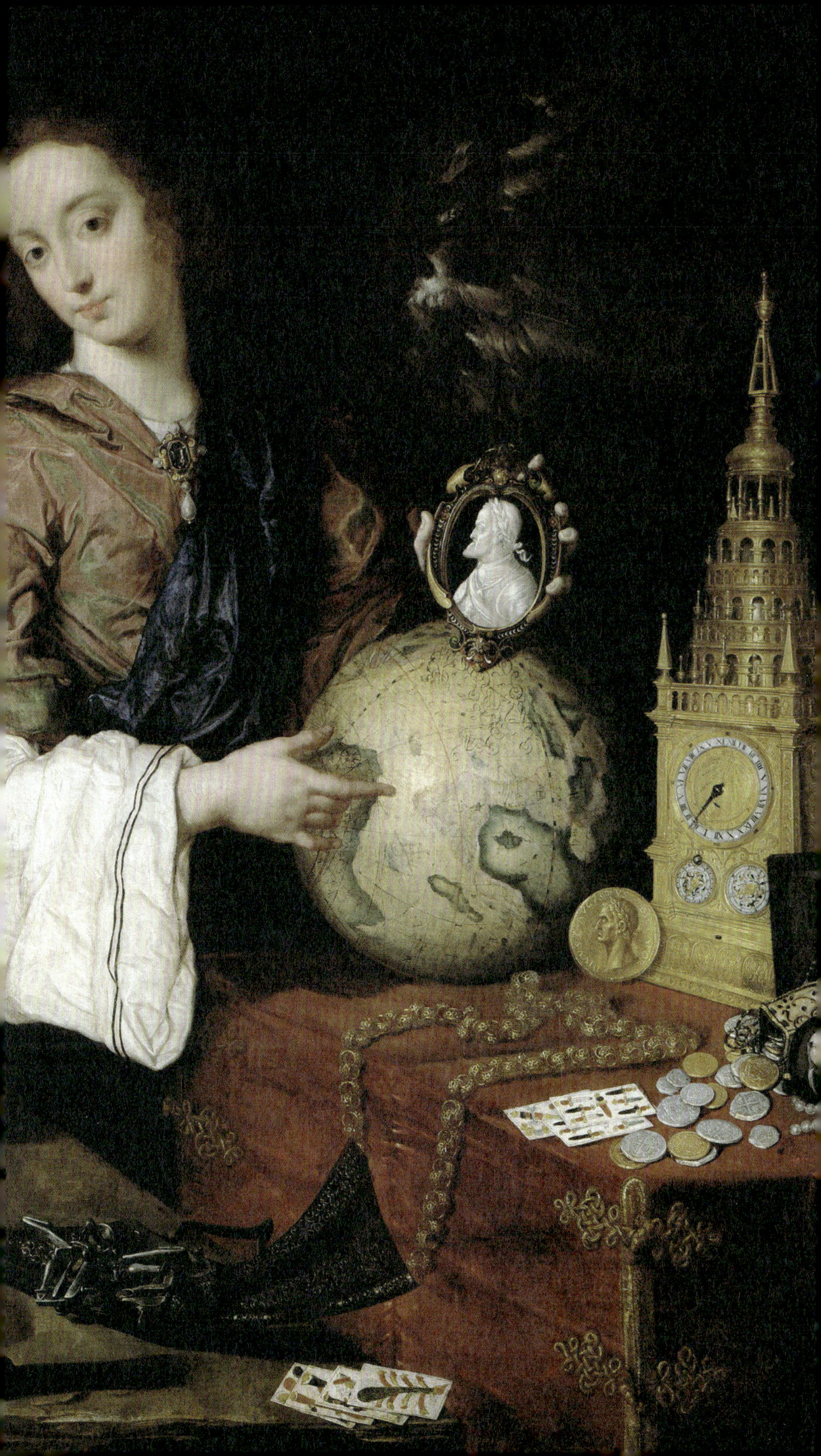

Do not act as if you had ten thousand years to throw away. Death stands at your elbow. Be good for something while you live and it is in your power.

——**Marcus Aurelius** 121-180 : *Meditations*

生死,人生歷程的始末

不要活得好似有萬年時光可虛擲。死亡近在咫尺。只要你活著、而且還能掌握事態，隨時準備好應對任何事。

—— 奧里略《沉思錄》

The fear of death follows from the fear of life. A man who lives fully is prepared to die at any time.

——**Mark Twain** 1835-1910

生死，人生歷程的始末

對死的恐懼尾隨著對生的畏懼而來。一個活得徹底的人早已準備好隨時死去。

—— 馬克・吐溫

Death will come in any case, and there is a long afterwards if the priests are right and nothing to fear if they are wrong.

——**Graham Greene** 1904-1991 : *The Honorary Consul*

生死，人生歷程的始末

死亡無論如何都會到來。牧師如果說的對,那麼死後還會有很多時間;如果他們是錯的,那麼也就沒什麼好怕的。

—— 葛林《名譽領事》

I have no idea what's awaiting me, or what will happen when this all ends. For the moment I know this: there are sick people and they need curing.

——**Albert Camus** 1913-1960 : *The Plague*

生死，人生歷程的始末

我不知道什麼在等著我,或是這一切結束之後會發生什麼。在這一刻,我只知道:有人生病,他們需要醫治。

—— 卡繆《瘟疫》

Men fear death as children fear to go in the dark; and as that natural fear in children is increased with tales, so is the other.

——**Francis Bacon** 1561-1626 : *Essays 'Of Death'*

生死,人生歷程的始末

人怕死,就像孩童害怕走進黑暗;而就如孩童與生俱來的恐懼會隨著聽來的故事滋長,成人對於死亦如是。

―― 培根〈論死亡〉

生死，人生歷程的始末

BOOK OF DEATH

Growing up is losing some illusions, in order to acquire others.

——**Virginia Woolf** 1882-1941

生死，人生歷程的始末

成長就是失去某些幻覺，以便獲取其他幻覺。

—— 吳爾芙

If you want to make God laugh, tell him about your plans.

——**Woody Allen** 1935-

生死,人生歷程的始末

你如果想逗上帝發笑,就把你的盤算告訴祂。

—— 伍迪・艾倫

For to fear death, my friends, is only to think ourselves wise without really being wise, for it is to think that we know what we do not know. For no one knows whether death may not be the greatest good that can happen to man.

—— **Plato** 427-347 BC : *Apology*

至於畏懼死亡，我的朋友啊，那只是我們在自作聰明，因為那是我們自以為懂得我們並不了解的事物。沒人知道死亡是否是能發生在人類身上最美善的一件事。

—— 柏拉圖《申辯篇》

Take it moment by moment, and you will find that we are all, as I've said before, bugs in amber.

——**Kurt Vonnegut** 1922-2007 : *Slaughterhouse-Five*

生死,人生歷程的始末

一步一步來,你將發現,我們就如我先前所說,全都是琥珀裡的昆蟲。

—— 馮內果《第五號屠宰場》

We fear death, we shudder at life's instability, we grieve to see the flowers wilt again and again, and the leaves fall, and in our hearts we know that we, too, are transitory and will soon disappear. When artists create pictures and thinkers search for laws and formulate thoughts, it is in order to salvage something from the great dance of death, to make something last longer than we do.

——**Hermann Hesse** 1877-1962 : *Narcissus and Goldmund*

生死，人生歷程的始末

我們畏懼死亡，我們因生命無常而顫抖，我們為眼見花凋葉落次次復次次而哀傷，我們深知己壽同樣短暫無常，轉瞬即逝。藝術家創造圖像、思想家探求思想的原理與公式，都是為了從死亡宏大的舞姿底下挽救某些事物，讓它們持存得比我們更長久。

—— **赫塞**《知識與愛情》

Don't look forward to the day you stop suffering, because when it comes you'll know you're dead.

——**Tennessee Williams** 1911-1983

生死，人生歷程的始末

莫期待你不再受苦的那天,因為當那天來臨,你將明白自己已死。

——田納西・威廉斯

We do not die because we have to die; we die because one day, and not so long ago, our consciousness was forced to deem it necessary.

——**Antonin Artaud** 1896-1948

生死，人生歷程的始末

我們還沒死,是因為我們必須死;而我們會死,是因為從某天起,就在不久之前,我們的意識被迫將死亡視作必然。

——法國詩人、劇場理論家亞陶

The rest of my days I'm going to spend on the sea. And when I die, I'm going to die on the sea. You know what I shall die of? I shall die of eating an unwashed grape. One day out on the ocean I will die—with my hand in the hand of some nice looking ship's doctor, a very young one with a small blond moustache and a big silver watch. "Poor lady," they'll say, "The quinine did her no good. That unwashed grape has transported her soul to heaven."

——**Tennessee Williams** 1911-1983 : *A Streetcar Named Desire*

我將把餘生耗在海上。這樣，我死時就會死在海上。你知道我會因什麼而死嗎？我會因吃下一顆沒洗過的葡萄而死。有一天，我將在航向大海時死去——我的手會被某個好看的船醫牽起，他留著一小撮金色八字鬍，戴著一大只的銀色手錶，非常年輕。「可憐的女士，」他們會這麼說，「奎寧也救不了她。那顆沒洗過的葡萄將她的靈魂送上了天堂。」

——田納西‧威廉斯《欲望街車》

Death is stronger than life, it pulls like a wind through the dark, all our cries burlesqued in joyless laughter; and with the garbage of loneliness stuffed down us until our guts burst bleeding green, we go screaming round the world, dying in our rented rooms, nightmare hotels, eternal homes of the transient heart.

——**Truman Capote** 1924-1984 : *Other Voices, Other Rooms*

生死,人生歷程的始末

死亡比生命來得強而有力，它如一陣巡過暗處的風摧枯拉朽，讓我們的每一聲哭泣都滑稽得有如冷笑；揣著那些硬塞進我們內裡、直逼膽囊泌出青汁的寂寞垃圾，我們在整個世界裡頭尖叫，在這顆朝生暮死之心賃居的房間、夢魘般的飯店、永恆的歸宿當中死去。

——楚門・卡波提《其他聲音，其他房間》

生死，人生歷程的始末

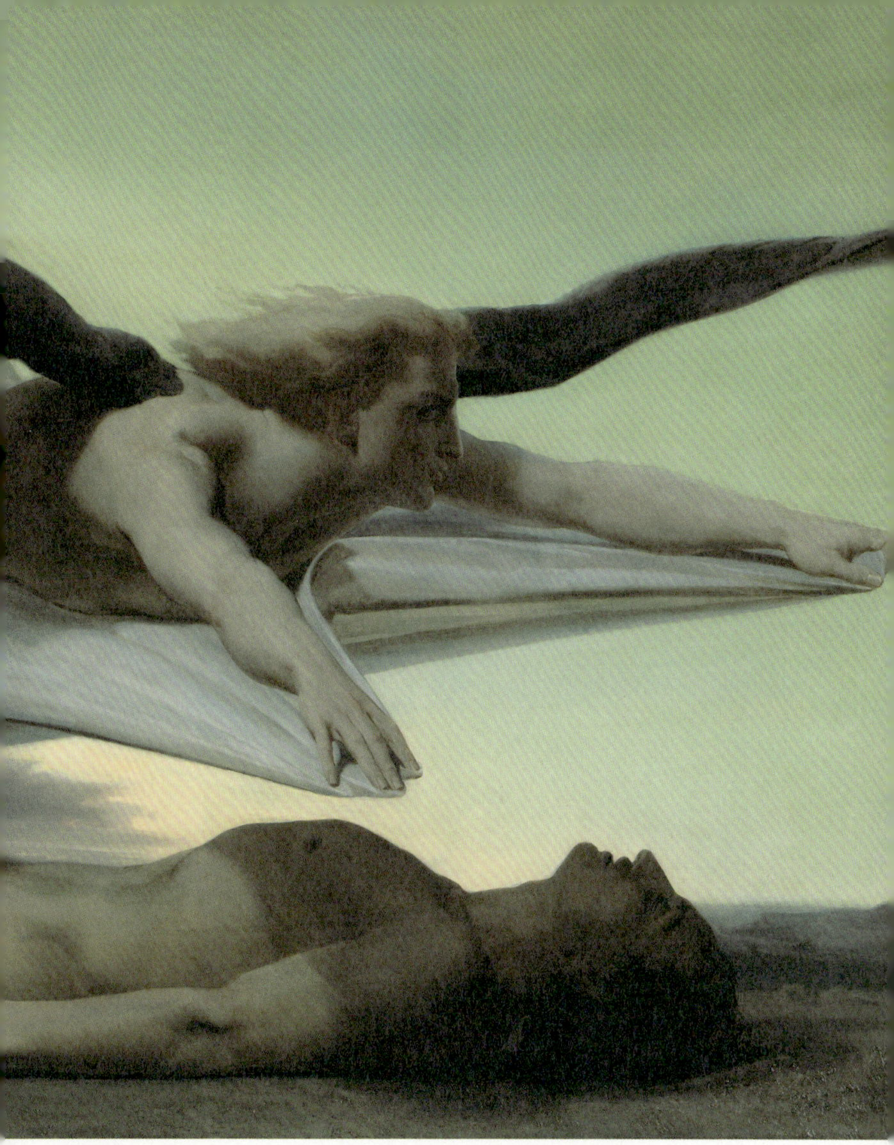

III

通往死寂的單程票

Of all the ways to lose a person, death is the kindest.

——**Ralph Waldo Emerson** 1803-1882

生死,人生歷程的始末

在失去一個人的所有方式中，死亡是最仁慈的。

—— 愛默生

The darkness of death is like the evening twilight; it makes all objects appear more lovely to the dying.

——**Jean Paul** 1763-1825

生死,人生歷程的始末

死亡的陰影就像黃昏的暮色；它讓所有事物對垂死之人而言顯得更加可愛。

—— 德國作家尚・保羅

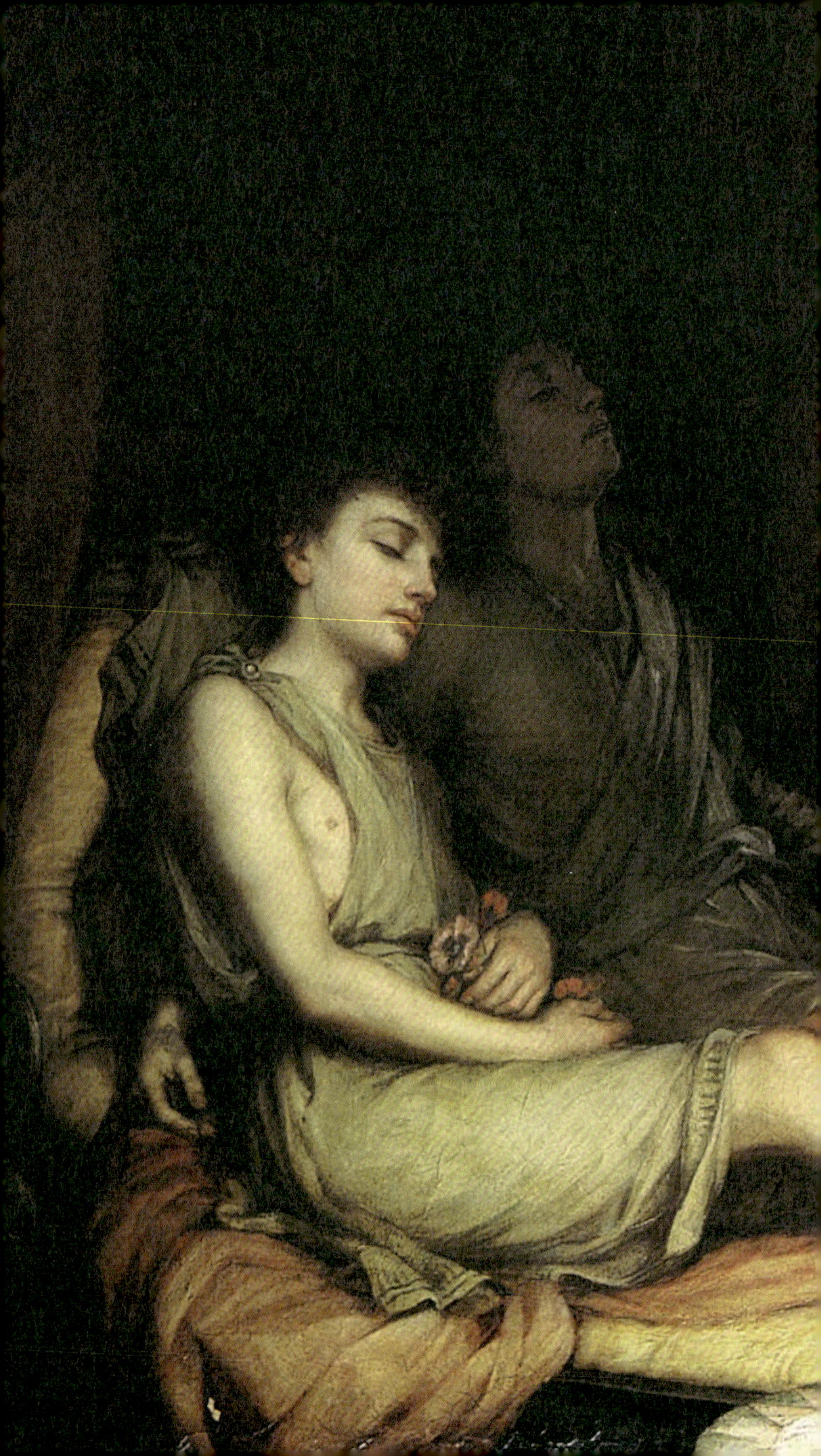

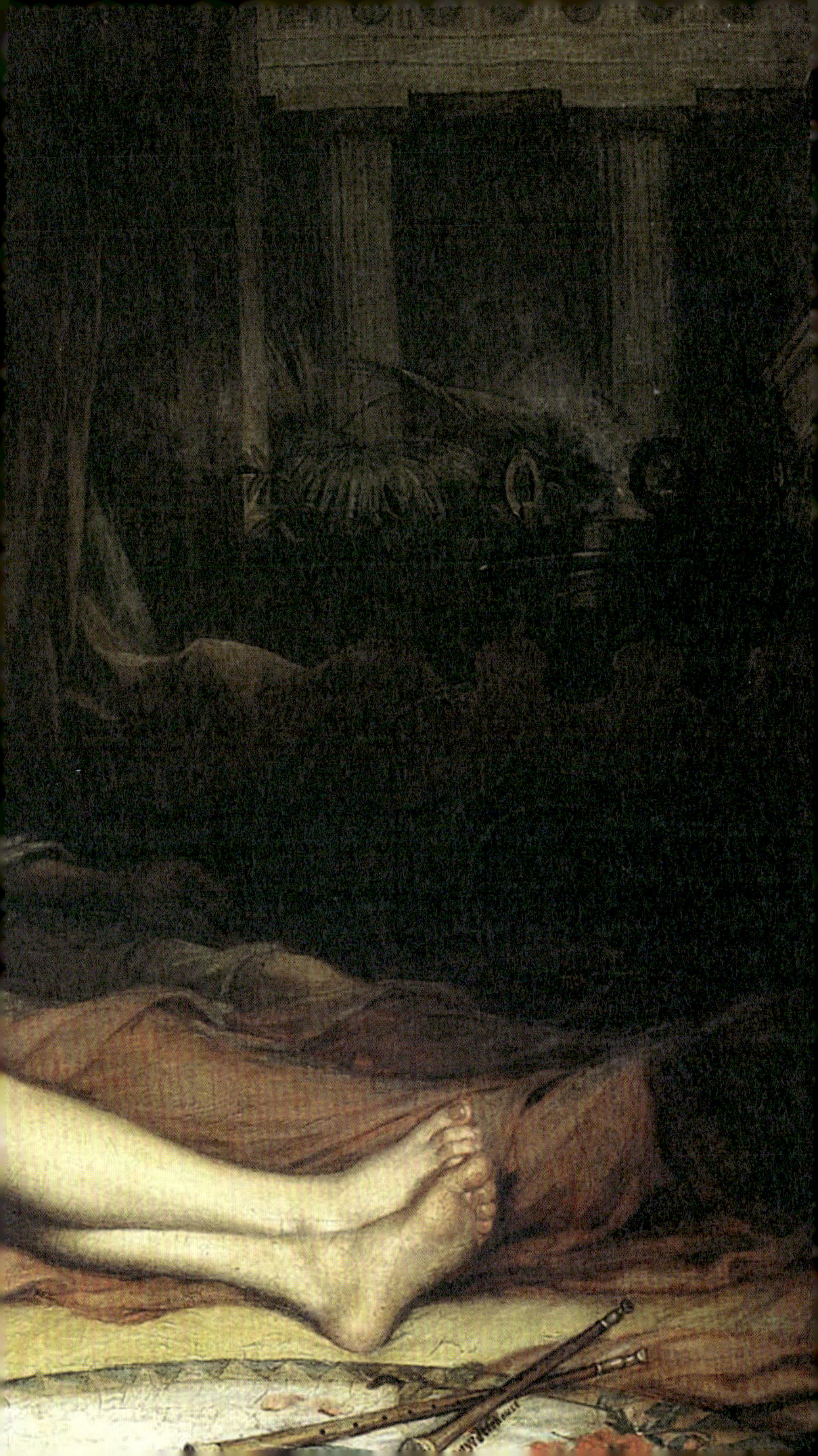

Death smiles at us all, all a man can do is smile back.

——**Marcus Aurelius** 121-180 : *Meditations*

生死，人生歷程的始末

死亡向我們投以一哂，凡人也僅能報以一笑。

—— 奧里略《沉思錄》

Death is a friend of ours; and he that is not ready to entertain him is not at home.

—— **Francis Bacon** 1561-1626 : *Sylva Sylvarum*

死是我們的朋友;還沒準備好取悅他的人才會感到不自在。

　　——培根《木林集》

End and Goal: Not every end is a goal. The end of a melody is not its goal: but nonetheless, had the melody not reached its end it would not have reached its goal either. A parable.

——**Friedrich Nietzsche** 1844-1900 : *Human, All Too Human*

終點與目的:並非所有終點都是目的。一段旋律的目的並非到達終點:但旋律若未達到終點,那它也不會達成目的。依此類推。

—— 尼采《人性的,太人性的》

Death is the veil which those who live call life: They sleep, and it is lifted.

——**Percy Bysshe Shelley** 1792-1822 : *Prometheus Unbound*

生死，人生歷程的始末

死是生者稱為生命的那層面紗:當他們沉睡,面紗便被掀起。

—— 雪萊《獲釋的普羅米修斯》

For this moment, this one moment, we are together. I press you to me. Come, pain, feed on me. Bury your fangs in my flesh. Tear me asunder. I sob, I sob.

——**Virginia Woolf** 1882-1941: *The Waves*

生死,人生歷程的始末

這一刻,就這一刻,我們同在。我將你按向胸口。來吧,痛苦,享用我。將你的獠牙深深埋進我的血肉。將我撕得四分五裂。我啜泣,我啜泣。

—— 吳爾芙《海浪》

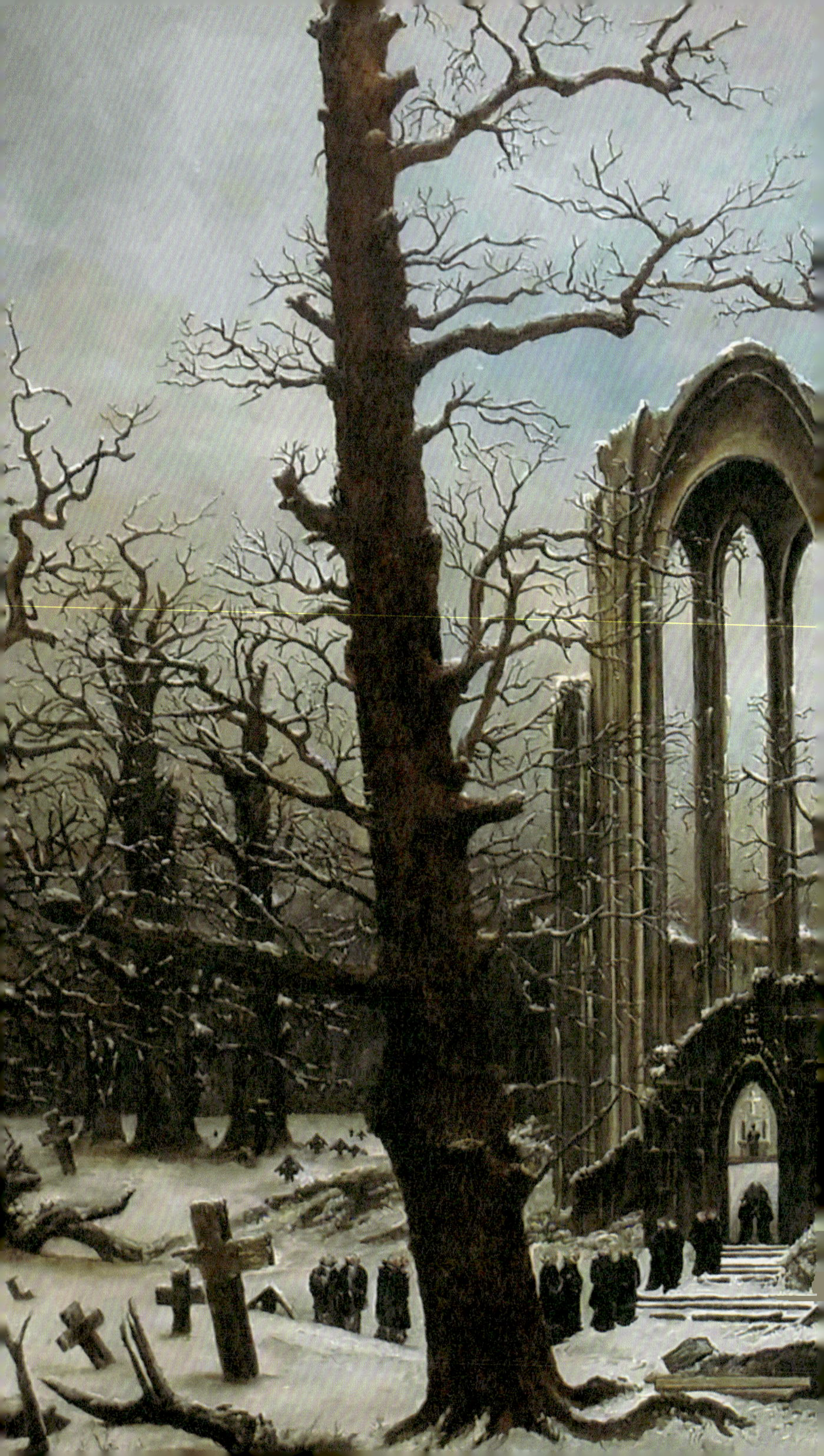

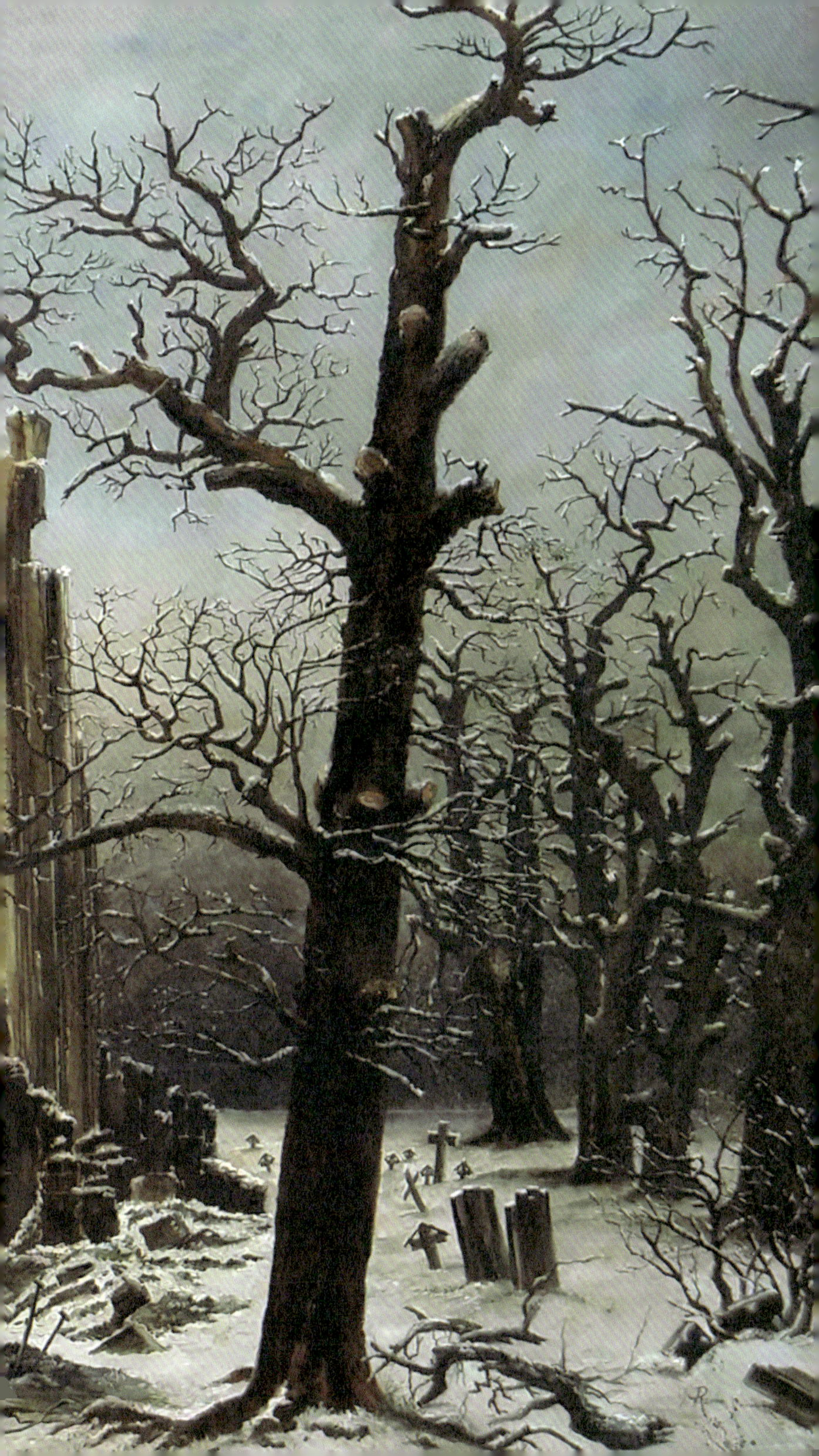

I'm not afraid of death; I just don't want to be there when it happens.

——**Woody Allen** 1935- : *Death*

生死，人生歷程的始末

我並不怕死;只是當它發生時我不想在場。

　　──伍迪・艾倫《死亡》

When the body sinks into death, the essence of man is revealed. Man is a knot, a web, a mesh into which relationships are tied. Only those relationships matter. The body is an old crock that nobody will miss. I have never known a man to think of himself when dying. Never.

——**Antoine de Saint-Exupéry** 1900-1944 : *Pilote de guerre*

當肉體沒入死亡之中，人的本質才獲揭露。人是一道結、一張網、一張所有關係皆繫於其上的網。只有這些關係才重要。肉體是老舊廢物，沒人會懷念。我從不知道有誰在死時會想起他自己。從不。

—— 聖修伯里《戰鬥的飛行員》

When you came you cried and everybody smiled with joy; when you go smile and let the world cry for you.

——**Rabindranath Tagore** 1861-1941

生死,人生歷程的始末

當你呱呱墜地,所有人洋溢笑臉歡喜迎你到來;當你含笑而去,整個世界哭送你離開。

—— 泰戈爾

生死，人生歷程的始末

Stipendium peccati
MORS

Hodie mihi cras tibi.

Cum morietur homo, hæreditabit serpentes & bestias, et Vermes *Eccl.* Als die menschen sterven, serpenten, bestien in wormen sy erven.

Vrsuchtigeitt wollust vnd pracht	Luxus, deliciæ, pompaque sæculi,	Ioye delices, du monde caresses
Die edilheit vnd Kleider dracht	Fasces, nobilitas, Stemmata, purpura,	Des Princes couronnes, renomineés, noblesses
Grosse namen reichtum vnd macht	Nomen, diuitiæ, fluxaq́ gloria,	Fame estendue richesses et puissance
Ist nur allein ein draum der nacht.	Ecquid sunt aliud, quà breue somniū?	Ques aultre, q'un someil et vain ioyssance
Der dodt ist allen gantz gewiss	Certo veniunt ordine Parcæ,	La MORT par my le monde voyageant
Keinner ist frey von seinen biss,	Nulli iusso cessare licet,	L'heure et le iour destine va finissant
Den doodt entgen Keiner Kan	Nulli scriptum proferre diem,	Nulle persone la peult certes eschapper
Ehr sey ein iont Oder ein man.	Recipit populos vrna citatos.	Aprens a mourir pendant tu peus respirer

G. Altzenbach exc.

BOOK OF DEATH

Life...is a tale
Told by an idiot, full of sound and fury,
Signifying nothing.

———**William Shakespeare** 1564-1616 : *Macbeth*

生死，人生歷程的始末

生命……是一則廢話
由白痴所述,喧囂而憤怒,
言之卻無物。

—— 莎士比亞《馬克白》

Do not wait for the last judgment. It comes every day.

——**Albert Camus** 1913-1960 : *The Fall*

生死,人生歷程的始末

毋庸等待最後的審判。它每天都在降臨。

—— 卡繆《墮落》

When you're dead, they really fix you up. I hope to hell when I do die somebody has sense enough to just dump me in the river or something. Anything except sticking me in a goddam cemetery. People coming and putting a bunch of flowers on your stomach on Sunday, and all that crap. Who wants flowers when you're dead? Nobody.

——**J.D. Salinger** 1919-2010 : *The Catcher in the Rye*

生死，人生歷程的始末

當你死時，別人真的會把你打點得很好。我真他媽的希望我死後有人觀念夠好，可以直接把我丟進河裡之類的。就是別把我埋到天殺的墓園裡。大家禮拜天會過來在我肚子放上一束花，還有其他這等的狗屎。誰死後還會想要花？沒有人。

—— **沙林傑**《麥田捕手》

Dying is the most embarrassing thing that can ever happen to you, because someone's got to take care of all your details.

——**Andy Warhol** 1928-1987 : *America*

生死,人生歷程的始末

死去是可能發生在你身上最窘困的事,因為有其他人會接管你的一切細節。

—— 安迪・沃荷《美國》

Even in the grave, all is not lost.

—— **Edgar Allan Poe** 1809-1849 : *The Gold-Bug*

生死，人生歷程的始末

就算進了墳墓,什麼也丟不掉。

—— 愛倫坡《金甲蟲》

To the living we owe respect, but to the dead we owe only the truth.

——**Voltaire** 1694-1778 : *letter to M. de Genonville*

於生者我們有欠體貼,但於死者我們只欠真相。

—— **伏爾泰,致杰農維爾書信**

Only where there are graves are there resurrections.

——**Friedrich Nietzsche** 1844-1900 : *Also sprach Zarathustra*

生死，人生歷程的始末

有墳墓的地方才有復活。

——尼采《查拉圖斯特拉如是說》

Life is pleasant. Death is peaceful. It's the transition that's troublesome.

——**Isaac Asimov** 1920-1992

生死，人生歷程的始末

生愉悅、死平靜。麻煩的是生死之間的過渡。

―― 艾西莫夫

The boundaries which divide Life from Death are at best shadowy and vague. Who shall say where the one ends, and where the other begins?

——**Edgar Allan Poe** 1809-1849 : *The Premature Burial*

生死,人生歷程的始末

分隔生與死的界線至多是模糊而朦朧的。誰能斷言一者在哪裡結束，而另一者又從何處開始？

—— **愛倫坡** 《過早的埋葬》

I never understood why when you died, you didn't just vanish, everything should just keep going on the way it was only you just wouldn't be there. I always thought I'd like my own tombstone to be blank. No epitaph, and no name. Well, actually, I'd like it to say 'figment'.

——**Andy Warhol** 1928-1987 : *America*

生死，人生歷程的始末

我永遠不懂，人死了之後為何不能徹底消失就好，而其他一切都照常運作，只是你不在那裡而已。我一直在想，希望自己的墓碑上一片空白。沒有碑文、沒有名姓。好吧，其實我希望上面寫著「純屬虛構」。

——安迪・沃荷《美國》

And you know, there's less charm in life when you think about death—but it's more peaceful.

—— **Leo Tolstoy** 1828-1910 : *Anna Karenina*

生死,人生历程的始末

你也知道,當你想到死亡,生命就少了一點魅力——但卻多了一分平靜。

——**托爾斯泰**《安娜‧卡列尼娜》

There is nothing frightening about an eternal dreamless sleep. Surely it is better than eternal torment in Hell and eternal boredom in Heaven.

——**Isaac Asimov** 1920-1992 : *I, Asimov: A Memoir*

生死，人生歷程的始末

無夢的永眠沒什麼好怕的。這當然好過地獄無盡的折磨與天堂永恆的無趣。

—— 艾西莫夫《我,艾西莫夫:回憶錄》

Life is for the living.
Death is for the dead.
Let life be like music.
And death a note unsaid.

——**Langston Hughes** 1902-1967 : *The Collected Poems*

生死，人生歷程的始末

生即予生者。
死即予死者。
若生命有如樂聲。
死就是無語音符。

—— 朗斯頓・休斯《詩集》

From my rotting body, flowers shall grow and I am in them, and that is eternity.

——**Edvard Munch** 1863-1944 : *In a unpublished scrapbook*

生死,人生歷程的始末

從我的朽爛屍身有花而生,而我存乎其中,此即永恆。

——畫家孟克,寫於未發表的剪貼本

Wherever you feel death, feel it. Don't escape. Death is beautiful; death is the greatest mystery, more mysterious than life. Through life you can gain the world, the futile world—meaningless, worthless. Through death you can gain the eternal. Death is the door.

——**Osho** 1931-1990 : *Sex Matters: From Sex to Superconsciousness*

只要你感受到死亡,就好好感受。不要逃避。死亡是美麗的;死亡是至高的神祕,遠比生命還要神祕。透過生命你能得到世界,無關緊要的世界 —— 毫無意義、毫無價值。透過死亡你能得到永恆。死亡就是那扇門。

—— **奧修**《從性到超意識》

It might be possible that the world itself is without meaning.

——**Virginia Woolf** 1882-1941 : *Mrs. Dalloway*

生死,人生歷程的始末

這個世界可能本身就毫無意義。

—— 吳爾芙《戴洛維夫人》

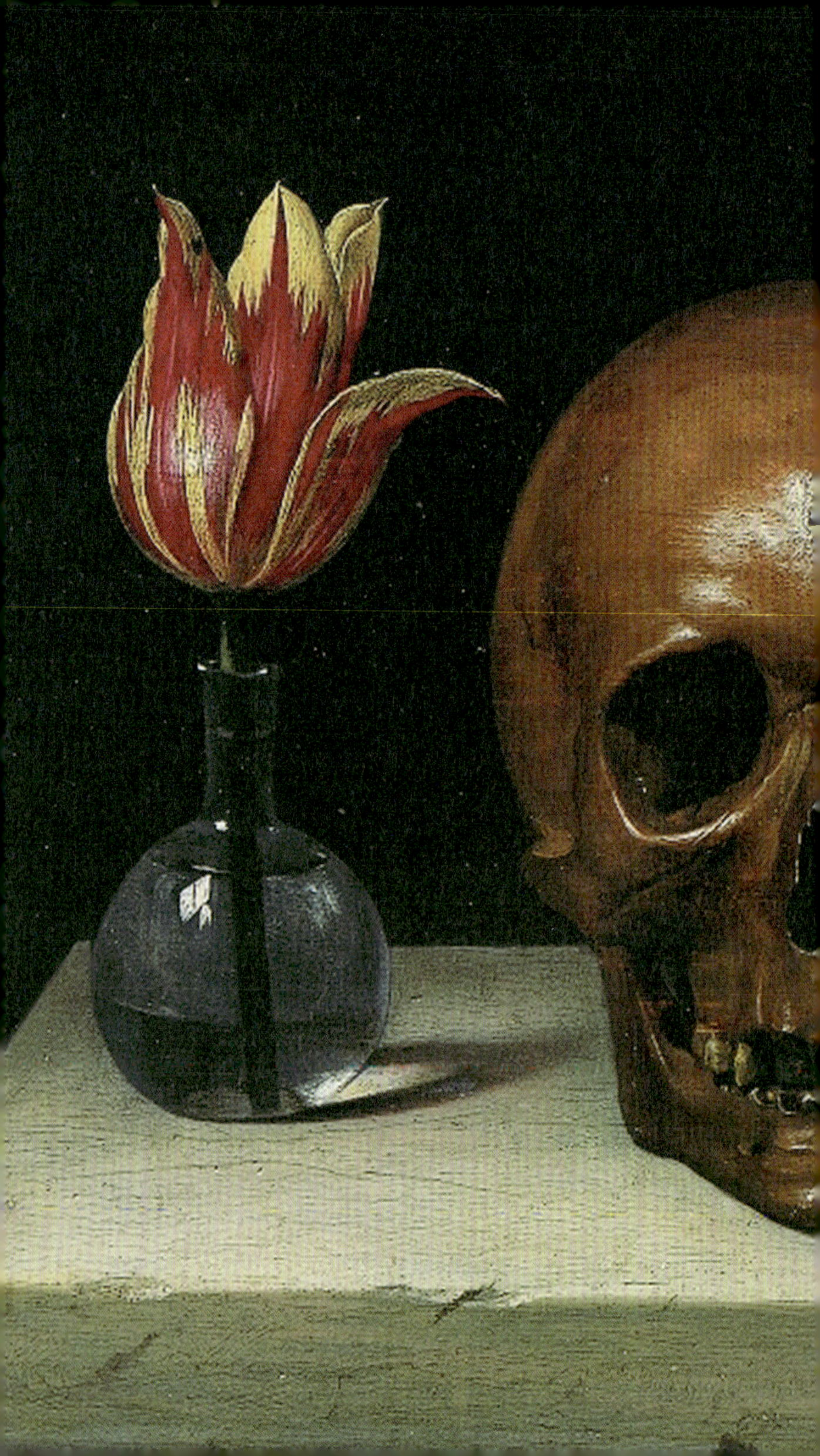

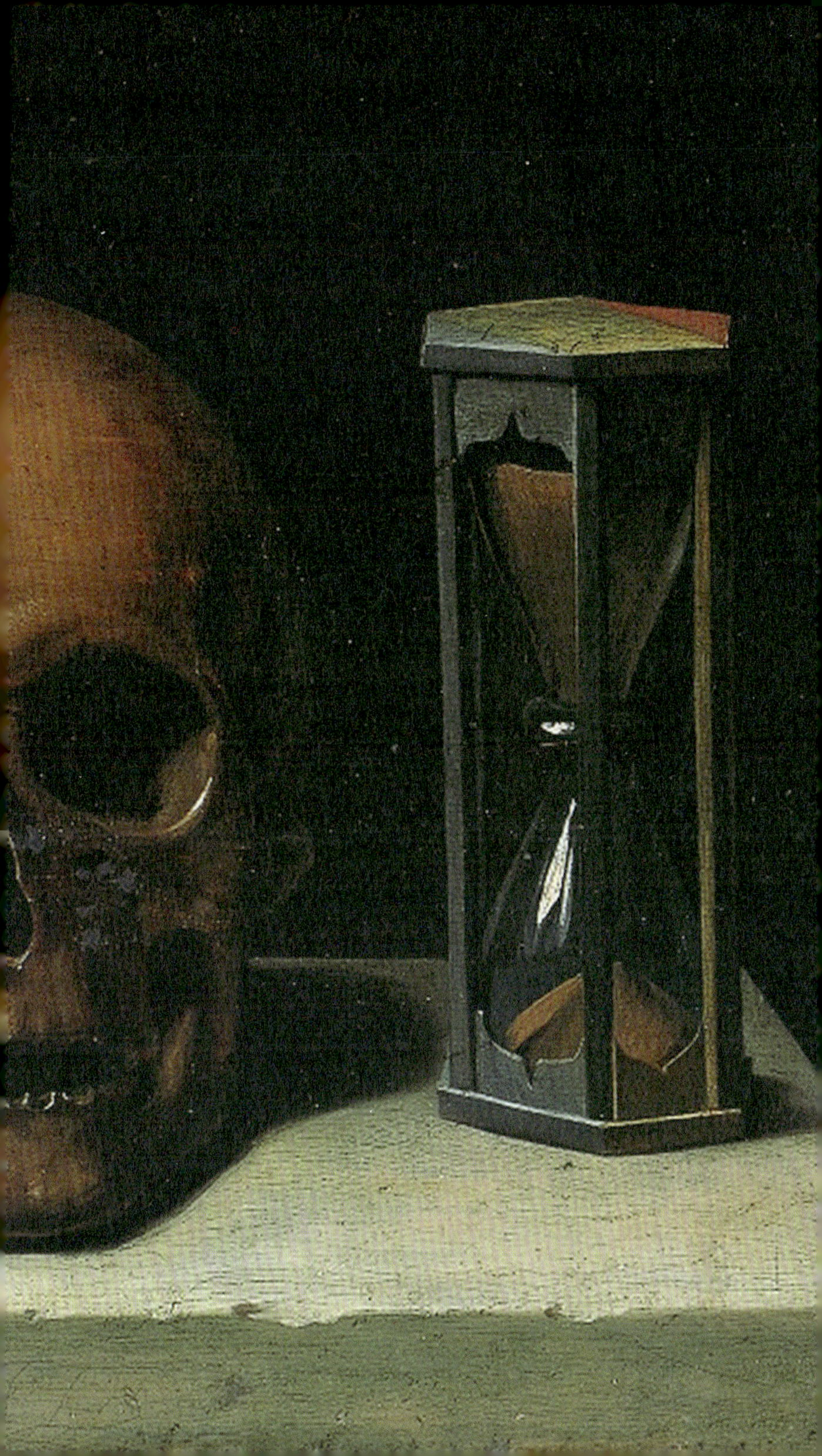

IV

精神綠洲

A single death is a tragedy; a million deaths is a statistic.

——**Joseph Stalin** 1878-1953

生死，人生歷程的始末

一個人的死是一場悲劇；一百萬個人的死是一條數據。

——史達林

Death is the wish of some, the relief of many, and the end of all.

——**Lucius Annaeus Seneca** c. 4 BC-AD 65

生死,人生歷程的始末

死亡是某些人的心願、多數人的寬慰，以及所有人的結局。

──塞內卡

Our life is made by the death of others.

——**Leonardo da Vinci** 1452-1519 : *'Anatomy, Zoology and Physiology'*

生死，人生歷程的始末

他人的死造就我們的生。

―― **達文西**〈解剖學,動物學及生理學筆記〉

If souls survive death for all eternity, how can the heavens hold them all? Or for that matter, how can the earth hold all the bodies that have been buried in it? The answers are the same. Just as on earth, with the passage of time, decaying and transmogrified corpses make way for the newly dead, so souls released into the heavens, after a season of flight, begin to break up, burn, and be absorbed back into the womb of reason, leaving room for souls just beginning to fly. This is the answer for those who believe that souls survive death.

——**Marcus Aurelius** 121-180 : *Meditations*

如果死後靈魂還能永恆不滅,天堂怎麼可能將之盡數納入?又或者,土地怎麼可能容得下所有入土的屍體?這兩者的答案是一樣的。一如地面上的屍骸隨時間推移日漸腐毀,讓位給新來的死者,釋入天堂的靈魂一樣在短暫飛行後隨即崩解、燃燒,自然而然地被子宮吸收回去,為正要飛起的其他魂魄騰出空間 —— 這就是說給那些相信死後靈魂不滅的人聽的答案。

—— 奧里略《沉思錄》

One by one they were all becoming shades. Better pass boldly into that other world, in the full glory of some passion, than fade and wither dismally with age.

——**James Joyce** 1882-1941 : *'The Dead'*, *Dubliners*

生死，人生歷程的始末

他們一個接著一個全變成暗影。比起隨著流光慘淡地褪色、凋零，進入另一個世界時最好帶著膽量，浸身在某中激情的榮光之中。

—— 喬伊斯《都柏林人》〈死者〉

生死，人生歷程的始末

BOOK OF DEATH

Neither the sun nor death can be looked at steadily.

——**François de La Rochefoucauld** 1613-1680 : *Maximes et Reflexions diverses*

生死,人生歷程的始末

驕陽與死亡,人皆無法直視。

—— 拉羅什福柯《人性箴言》

Life is a slope. As long as you're going up you're always looking towards the top and you feel happy, but when you reach it, suddenly you can see the road going downhill and death at the end of it all. It's slow going up and quick going down.

——**Guy de Maupassant** 1850-1893 : *Bel-Ami*

生死，人生歷程的始末

生命是一道斜坡。當你步步向上，你一直望向巔峰，心中喜悅；但當你抵達巔頂，突然卻只見前方道路直直落下，而死亡就在一切的盡頭。生命冉冉上升，而後急轉直下。

——莫泊桑《俊友》

To die is landing on some distant shore.

——**John Dryden** 1631-1700

生死，人生歷程的始末

死去是登上某個遙遠的彼岸。

──英國詩人約翰‧德萊頓

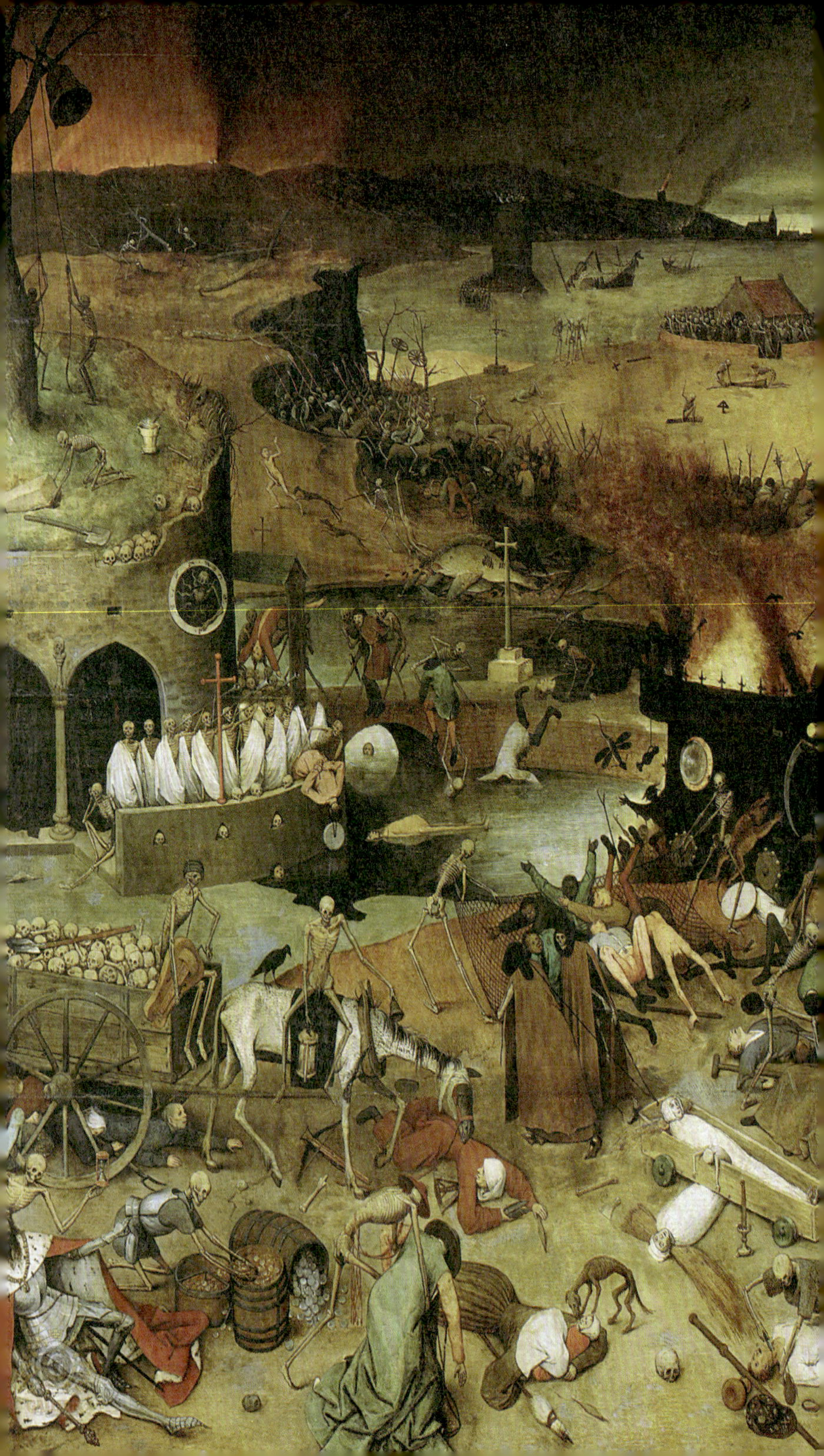

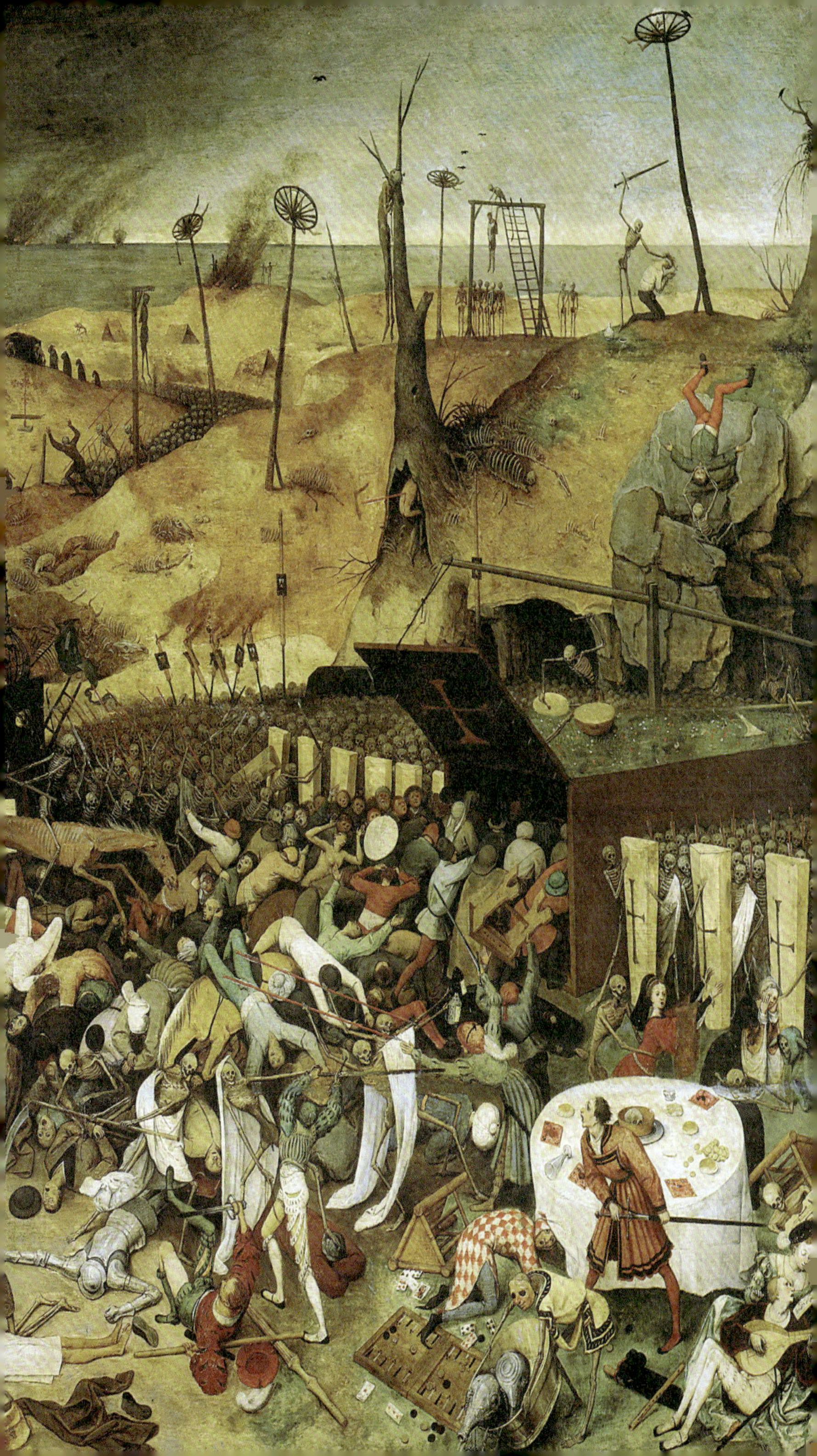

Each of us has his own rhythm of suffering.

——**Roland Barthes** 1915-1980 : *Journal de deuil*

生死，人生歷程的始末

我們都有各自受苦的步調。

——**羅蘭・巴特**《哀悼日記》

End? No, the journey doesn't end here. Death is just another path, one that we all must take. The grey rain-curtain of this world rolls back, and all turns to silver glass, and then you see it.

——**J.R.R. Tolkien** 1892-1973 : *The Lord of the Rings*

生死，人生歷程的始末

結束？不，這旅程並不在此結束。死亡不過是我們都得踏上的另一條小徑。此世的灰色雨幔褪去，盡數變成銀色玻璃，接著你會見到那條小徑。

—— **托爾金**《魔戒》

Death never takes a wise man by surprise; he is always ready to go.

———**Jean de la Fontaine** 1621-1695 : *Fables*

生死，人生歷程的始末

死亡從不出其不意地帶走智者;智者早已隨時準備好啟程。

—— 拉封丹《拉封丹寓言》

Death is nothing, but to live defeated and inglorious is to die daily.

——**Napoleon Bonaparte** 1769-1821

生死，人生歷程的始末

死亡不是大事,但活得挫敗且毫無尊嚴,則等同天天死去。

—— 拿破崙

What is called a reason for living is also an excellent reason for dying.

—— **Albert Camus** 1913-1960 : *The Myth of Sisyphus and Other Essays*

生死,人生歷程的始末

能被稱作生存理由的，也是去死的絕佳原因。

—— 卡繆《薛西弗斯的神話》

The whole life of the individual is nothing but the process of giving birth to himself; indeed, we should be fully born when we die—although it is the tragic fate of most individuals to die before they are born.

——**Erich Fromm** 1900-1980 : *The Sane Society*

獨立個體的一生不過是個體讓自己誕生的過程；的確，我們死去時應當要已完整地誕生 —— 儘管悲劇命運總讓多數人在真正出生之前就已死去。

—— 弗洛姆《健全社會》

If children were brought into the world by an act of pure reason alone, would the human race continue to exist? Would not a man rather have so much sympathy with the coming generation as to spare it the burden of existence, or at any rate not take it upon himself to impose that burden upon it in cold blood?

——**Arthur Schopenhauer** 1788-1860 : *Studies in Pessimism: The Essays*

如果孩子誕生於世僅是出於純粹理性的行為,那麼人類這個物種還能繼續存在嗎?一個對將來世代懷有高度同情的人,難道能不將存在的重擔分給他們嗎?又或者,再怎麼冷血而不願擔起存在重擔的人,能不將其加諸於下個世代之上嗎?

—— 叔本華《悲觀論集》

As a well-spent day brings happy sleep, so a life well spent brings happy death.

——**Leonardo da Vinci** 1452-1519 : *'Philosophy'*

日子有用自當睡得香甜,正如活出成果自當死得酣暢。

—— 達文西〈哲學筆記〉

If after I die, people want to write my biography, there is nothing simpler. They only need two dates: the date of my birth and the date of my death. Between one and another, every day is mine.

——**Fernando Pessoa** 1888-1935 : *Poems of Fernando Pessoa*

生死,人生歷程的始末

如果我死後有人想為我立傳，那真是再簡單不過的事。他們只需要兩個日期：我的出生日與我的死亡日。這兩個日期之間的每一天都是我的。

—— **佩索亞**《詩集》

And a thousand years from now man will still be sighing, "Oh! Life is so hard!" and will still, like now, be afraid of death and not want to die.

——**Anton Chekhov** 1860-1904 : *The Three Sisters*

生死，人生歷程的始末

而此去千年之後,人類將會繼續感嘆「噢,生活多苦啊!」也將如同現在繼續畏懼死亡,不願死去。

—— **契訶夫**《三姊妹》

The call of death is a call of love. Death can be sweet if we answer it in the affirmative, if we accept it as one of the great eternal forms of life and transformation.

——**Hermann Hesse** 1877-1962 : *letter, 1950*

生死，人生歷程的始末

死亡的召喚就是愛的召喚。如果我們肯定地回應它、接納它,視之如偉大永恆的生命形式與轉化,那麼死亡會是甜美的。

──赫塞,一九五〇年書信

Drink your tea slowly and reverently, as if it is the axis on which the world earth revolves—slowly, evenly, without rushing toward the future.

——**Thich Nhat Hanh** 1926- : *The Miracle of Mindfulness*

生死，人生歷程的始末

緩慢而恭敬地喝下手中茶，彷彿這杯茶是地球自轉的軸心——輕緩、寧靜、不急於奔向未來。

—— 一行禪師《正念的奇蹟》

生死，人生歷程的始末

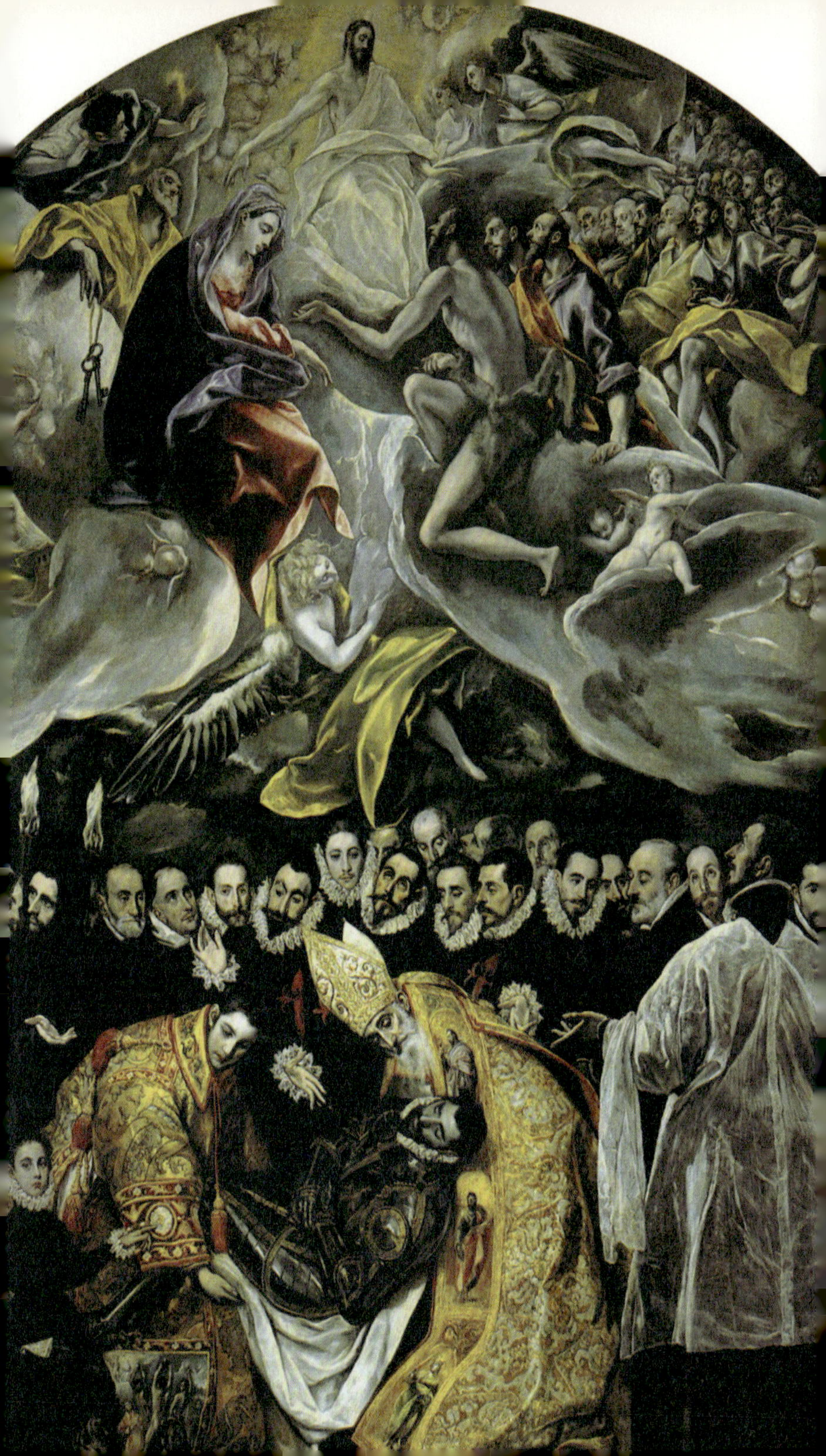

If you've never eaten while crying you don't know what life tastes like.

——**Johann Wolfgang von Goethe** 1749-1832

生死,人生歷程的始末

你若未曾含淚吃過飯，便不識生命是何滋味。

—— 歌德

There are only two ways to live your life. One is as though nothing is a miracle. The other is as though everything is a miracle.

——**Albert Einstein** 1879-1955

度過人生只有兩種方式：一種是彷彿世上沒有奇蹟，另一種是彷彿萬事萬物都是奇蹟。

—— 愛因斯坦

If you ask me what I came to do in this world, I, an artist, will answer you: I am here to live out loud.

——Émile Zola 1840-1902

生死，人生歷程的始末

你若問我來到這個世界所為何事，我，一介藝術家，將如此回答你：我來到這裡活出精彩。

——左拉

If I were to wish for anything, I should not wish for wealth and power, but for the passionate sense of the potential, for the eye which, ever young and ardent, sees the possible. Pleasure disappoints, possibility never. And what wine is so sparkling, what so fragrant, what so intoxicating, as possibility!

——**Søren Kierkegaard** 1813-1855 : *Either/Or*

如果我能許下任何願望,我不會選擇財富與權力,而會選擇潛然於事物的激情感受,以及那隻年輕而熾熱、能看見各種可能性的眼眸。歡快會令人失望,可能性卻從來不然。還有哪種酒比可能性來得更閃耀、更芳醇、更醉人呢?

—— 齊克果《非此即彼》

A life spent making mistakes is not only more honorable, but more useful than a life spent doing nothing.

——**George Bernard Shaw** 1856-1950 : *The Doctor's Dilemma*

生死,人生歷程的始末

一段耗在犯錯上的人生，不但比什麼都不做的人生來得光榮，甚至更為有用。

—— **蕭伯納**《醫生的兩難》

Life is a comedy to those who think, a tragedy to those who feel.

——**Horace Walpole** 1717-1797 : *Letter to Sir Horace Mann*

生死,人生歷程的始末

對思考者而言，人生是齣喜劇；對感受者而言，則是齣悲劇。

——英國作家渥波爾，致荷瑞斯曼爵士書信

Life is not a matter of holding good cards, but of playing a poor hand well.

——**Jack London** 1876-1916

生死，人生历程的始末

人生的重點不在於握有一手好牌,而在於打好手中的爛牌。

—— 傑克・倫敦

生死，人生歷程的始末

BOOK OF DEATH

V
置之死地，而後生

Every man's life ends the same way. It is only the details of how he lived and how he died that distinguish one man from another.

——**Ernest Hemingway** 1899-1961

生死，人生歷程的始末

每個人的生命都以相同方式結束。唯有曾經如何生活和如何死去的細節，才讓一個人有別於另一人。

—— 海明威

Be—don't try to become.

——**Osho** 1931-1990 : *The Book of Wisdom*

生死,人生歷程的始末

是你所是——不要試著成為你。

—— **奧修**《智慧之書》

It is not death that a man should fear, but he should fear never beginning to live.

——**Marcus Aurelius** 121-180 : *Meditations*

生死,人生歷程的始末

人該畏懼的不是死亡，而是從沒開始活著。

—— 奧里略《沉思錄》

生死，人生歷程的始末

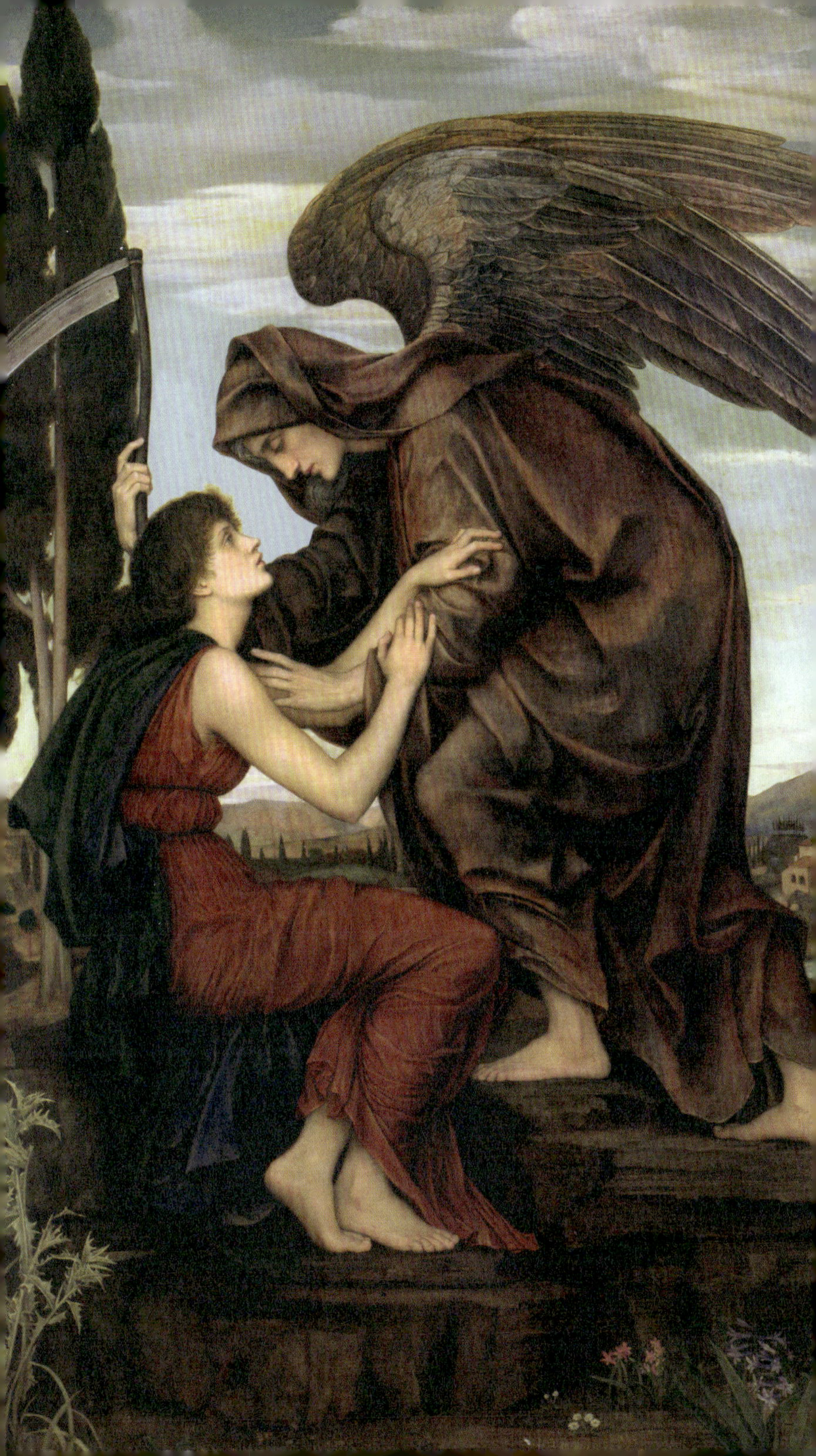

When we finally know we are dying, and all other sentient beings are dying with us, we start to have a burning, almost heartbreaking sense of the fragility and preciousness of each moment and each being, and from this can grow a deep, clear, limitless compassion for all beings.

—— **Sogyal Rinpoche** 1947- : *The Tibetan Book of Living and Dying*

生死，人生歷程的始末

當我們終於明白自己正邁向死亡,而其他一切有知覺的存在也會隨我們而逝,我們會開始對每一個當下的脆弱與珍貴產生一陣焦急、幾近心碎的感覺,而一種對萬物深沉、清明、無盡的憐憫之心遂由此而生。

——索甲仁波切《西藏生死書》

If your daily life seems poor, do not blame it; blame yourself, tell yourself that you are not poet enough to call forth its riches; for to the creator there is no poverty and no poor indifferent place.

——**Rainer Maria Rilke** 1875-1926 : *Letters to a Young Poet*

生死，人生歷程的始末

如果你的日常生活看似貧乏，別怪你的生活；怪你自己，告訴自己是你不夠詩意，因而召喚不出生活的豐足；因為對造物主而言，這世上沒有一處是荒蕪、漠然的貧乏之地。

──**里爾克**《致年輕詩人的信》

To live is the rarest thing in the world. Most people exist, that is all.

——**Oscar Wilde** 1854-1900 : *The Soul of Man Under Socialism*

生死，人生歷程的始末

世上罕有人真正活著，多數人只是存在，如此而已。

—— **王爾德**《社會主義下人的靈魂》

It seems to me that if you or I must choose between two courses of thought or action, we should remember our dying and try so to live that our death brings no pleasure to the world.

—— **John Steinbeck** 1902-1968 : *East of Eden*

生死,人生歷程的始末

對我來說，你我若是只能從兩套想法或行動之中擇一，那麼我們似乎應該惦記自己的死亡，並且嘗試如此過活，記得我們的死無法對世界帶來喜悅。

—— 史坦貝克《伊甸園東》

You are—your life, and nothing else.

——**Jean-Paul Sartre** 1905-1980 : *No Exit*

生死,人生歷程的始末

你僅是——你的人生,此外無他。

——**沙特**《無路可出》

It is nothing to die. It is frightful not to live.

——**Victor Hugo** 1802-1885 : *Les Misérables*

生死，人生歷程的始末

死不是問題，不活才真正駭人。

—— 雨果《悲慘世界》

As soon as you trust yourself, you will know how to live.

——**Johann Wolfgang von Goethe** 1749-1832 : *Faust: First Part*

生死,人生歷程的始末

一旦你信任自己,就會知道如何活著。

—— **歌德**《浮士德》第一部

It was a great mistake, my being born a man, I would have been much more successful as a seagull or a fish. As it is, I will always be a stranger who never feels at home, who does not really want and is not really wanted, who can never belong, who must be a little in love with death!

——**Eugene O'Neill** 1888-1953 : *Long Day's Journey Into Night*

生死，人生历程的始末

我生而為人實在是莫大錯誤，我若是海鷗或魚，活得或許還更成功。因此，我永遠都會是個格格不入的陌生人，既沒有真正想要什麼，也沒被誰真正想要過，從來得不到歸屬，而且必定對死亡稍稍傾心！

——尤金・歐尼爾《進入黑夜的漫長旅程》

I won't tell you that the world matters nothing, or the world's voice, or the voice of society. They matter a good deal. They matter far too much. But there are moments when one has to choose between living one's own life, fully, entirely, completely—or dragging out some false, shallow, degrading existence that the world in its hypocrisy demands. You have that moment now. Choose!

——**Oscar Wilde** 1854-1900 : *Lady Windermere's Fan*

我不會說這個世界或這世界的聲音、這個社會的聲音無關緊要。這些都事關重大。但人總有那麼一刻得作出選擇,是要完整、徹底地活出自己的人生,或是在這世界虛偽的要求下,虛假、膚淺、丟人現眼地苟延殘喘。你現在就面對著那麼一刻,選擇吧!

—— 王爾德《溫夫人的扇子》

生死，人生歷程的始末

BOOK OF DEATH

When the body escaped mutilation, seldom did the heart go to the grave unscarred.

——**Virginia Woolf** 1882-1941 : *Jacob's Room*

生死,人生歷程的始末

即使肉體能逃過損害,卻罕有心靈能毫髮無缺地進墳墓。

──吳爾芙《雅各的房間》

Life can only be understood backwards; but it must be lived forwards.

——**Søren Kierkegaard** 1813-1855 : *Journals, 1843*

生死，人生歷程的始末

人生只能往回理解,但必須朝前過活。

—— 齊克果,一八四三年日記

Enjoy life. There's plenty of time to be dead.

——**Hans Christian Andersen** 1805-1875

生死，人生歷程的始末

享受生命。你有很多時間能當死人。

—— 安徒生

My life didn't please me, so I created my life.

—— **Coco Chanel** 1883-1971

生死，人生歷程的始末

我的人生不合我意,所以我創造了自己的人生。

—— 香奈兒

One lives in the hope of becoming a memory.

———**Antonio Porchia** 1885-1968 : *Voces*

生死,人生歷程的始末

人活在成為回憶的希望當中。

—— 阿根廷詩人安東尼歐・玻契亞《遺忘的聲音》

生死，人生歷程的始末

BOOK OF DEATH

After a person dies, there is always something like a feeling of stupefaction, so difficult is it to comprehend this unexpected advent of nothingness and to resign oneself to believing it.

——**Gustave Flaubert** 1821-1880 : *Madame Bovary*

生死，人生歷程的始末

在他人死後,總有一陣麻木感油然而生,要理解這種不期而至的虛無,並甘心接受事實是何其困難。

—— **福樓拜**《包法利夫人》

Much have we loved you. But speechless was our love, and with veils has it been veiled.
Yet now it cries aloud unto you, and would stand revealed before you.
And ever has it been that love knows not its depth until the hour of separation.

——**Kahlil Gibran** 1883-1931 : *The Prophet*

生死,人生歷程的始末

我們多麼愛你。但我們的愛曾是無語，帷幕曾覆蓋其上。
現在這份愛對你高聲哭喊，在你面前無所遮掩。
而這種愛從不知道自己能有多深，直到別離的時刻來臨。

──**紀伯倫**《先知》

Our dead are never dead to us, until we have forgotten them.

—— **George Eliot** 1819-1880 : *Adam Bede*

生死，人生歷程的始末

死者從未真正死去,直到你我將他們遺忘。

——喬治・艾略特《亞當・畢德》

Mostly it is loss which teaches us about the worth of things.

——**Arthur Schopenhauer** 1788-1860 : *Parerga and Paralipomena*

大多時候,讓我們懂得事物價值的,正是失去。

—— **叔本華**《附錄與補遺》

They say, "The coward dies many times"; so does the beloved. Didn't the eagle find a fresh liver to tear in Prometheus every time it dined?

——**C.S. Lewis** 1898-1963 : *A Grief Observed*

人說,「懦夫早已死過不知幾回」;被愛者亦然。
老鷹每回啄食普羅米修斯之前,不也都先找到他的
鮮肝來撕裂嗎?

—— C. S. 路易士《卿卿如晤》

To forget the dead would be akin to killing them a second time.

——**Elie Wiesel** 1928-2016：*La Nuit*

遺忘死者猶如二度殺死他們。

—— 埃利・維瑟爾《夜》

Love never dies a natural death. It dies because we don't know how to replenish its source. It dies of blindness and errors and betrayals. It dies of illness and wounds; it dies of weariness, of witherings, of tarnishings.

——**Anaïs Nin** 1903-1977 : *The Four-Chambered Heart*

生死，人生歷程的始末

愛不會自然地終逝。愛會死去，是因為我們不知如何斟滿它的源頭。愛因盲目、犯錯與背叛而死。愛死於傷病與苦痛；愛死於磨耗、枯萎與黯淡。

——阿娜伊斯・寧《四腔室之心》

Live in my absence as if in a house.
Absence is a house so vast
that inside you will pass through its walls
and hang pictures on the air.
Absence is a house so transparent
that I, lifeless, will see you, living,
and if you suffer, my love, I will die again.

——**Pablo Neruda** 1904-1973 : *Sonnet XCIV*

生死,人生歷程的始末

活在我的離去之中,就像住在一幢屋子。
離去是如此碩大的一幢屋子
你將在裡頭穿越它的牆
將畫掛在空中。
離去是如此透明的一幢屋子
毫無生機的我,將眼睜睜看著你,活著,
而若你受了苦,我的摯愛,那我會再次死去。

—— **聶魯達**《情詩一百首》

If, then, I were asked for the most important advice I could give, that which I considered to be the most useful to the men of our century, I should simply say: in the name of God, stop a moment, cease your work, look around you.

——**Leo Tolstoy** 1828-1910 : *Essays, Letters and Miscellanies*

如果有人要我提供我所能給的最重要的建議，而且是我認為對這世紀的人最實用的一句話，我會簡單地說：看在上帝的份上，稍歇片刻，停下你的工作，看看你周遭吧。

—— **托爾斯泰**《散文、書信與雜集》

As death, when we come to consider it closely, is the true goal of our existence, I have formed during the last few years such close relationships with this best and truest friend of mankind that death's image is not only no longer terrifying to me, but is indeed very soothing and consoling, and I thank my God for graciously granting me the opportunity...of learning that death is the key which unlocks the door to our true happiness. I never lie down at night without reflecting that—young as I am—I may not live to see another day. Yet no one of all my acquaintances could say that in company I am morose or disgruntled.

——**Wolfgang Amadeus Mozart** 1956-1791 : *letter to Leopold Mozart, Apr. 4, 1787*

當我們仔細思量，死亡是我們存在的真正目標，過去幾年來我已經跟這位人類最好、最真誠的朋友建立起緊密的關係，因此死亡的形象已不再教我驚懼，反而讓我相當寬慰，而我感謝上帝慷慨地賜我這個機會……能學到死亡是開啟真正幸福大門的鑰匙。夜裡躺在床上時，我沒有一晚不會想到──即便年輕如我──也許我無法活著看到明天。然而，沒有朋友會說我在人前看起來抑鬱寡歡。

──莫札特，致父親書信，一七八七年四月四日

Life isn't about finding yourself. Life is about creating yourself.

——**George Bernard Shaw** 1856-1950

生死，人生歷程的始末

生命不在於找到你自己。生命在於創造你自己。

—— 蕭伯納

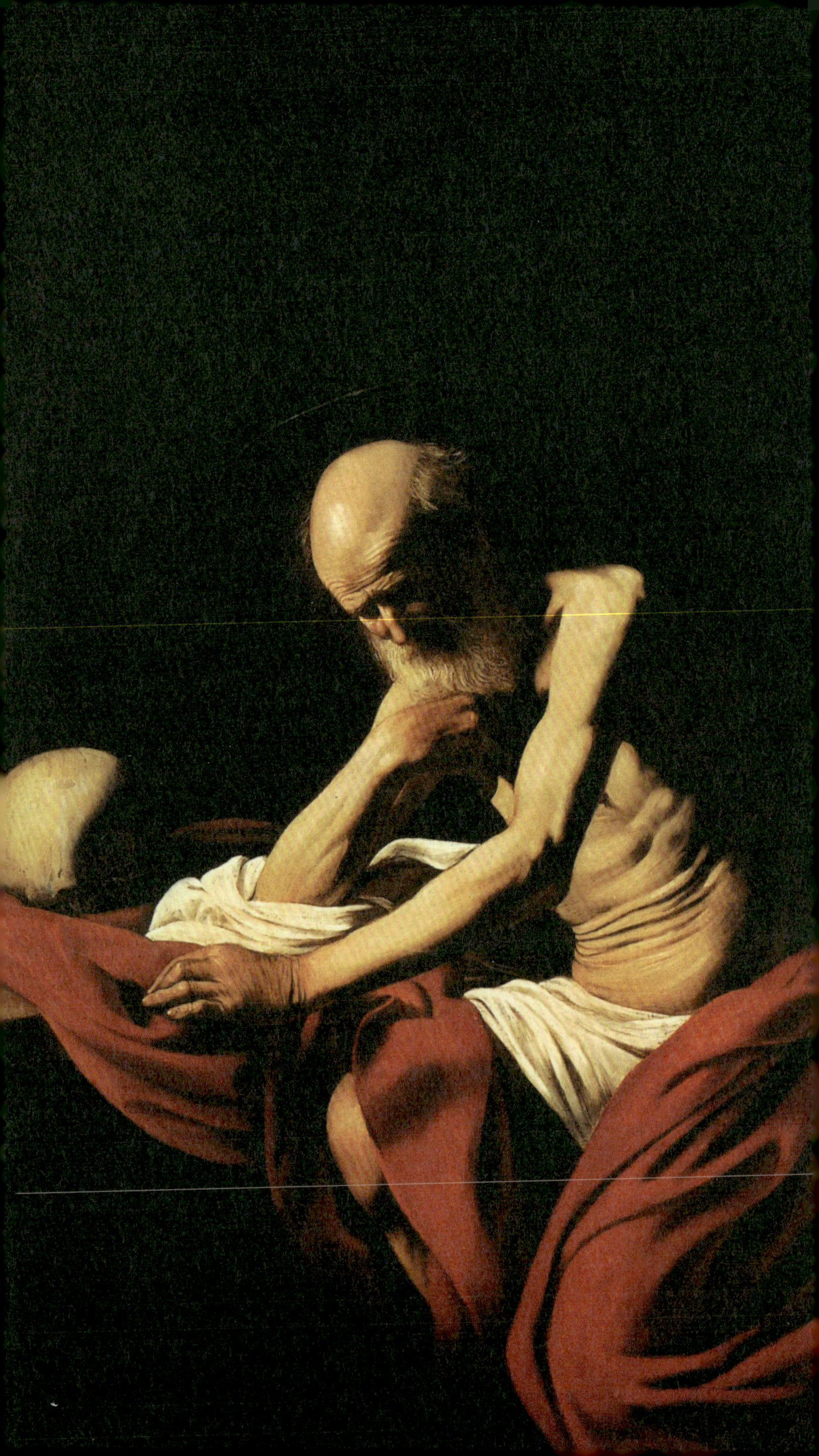

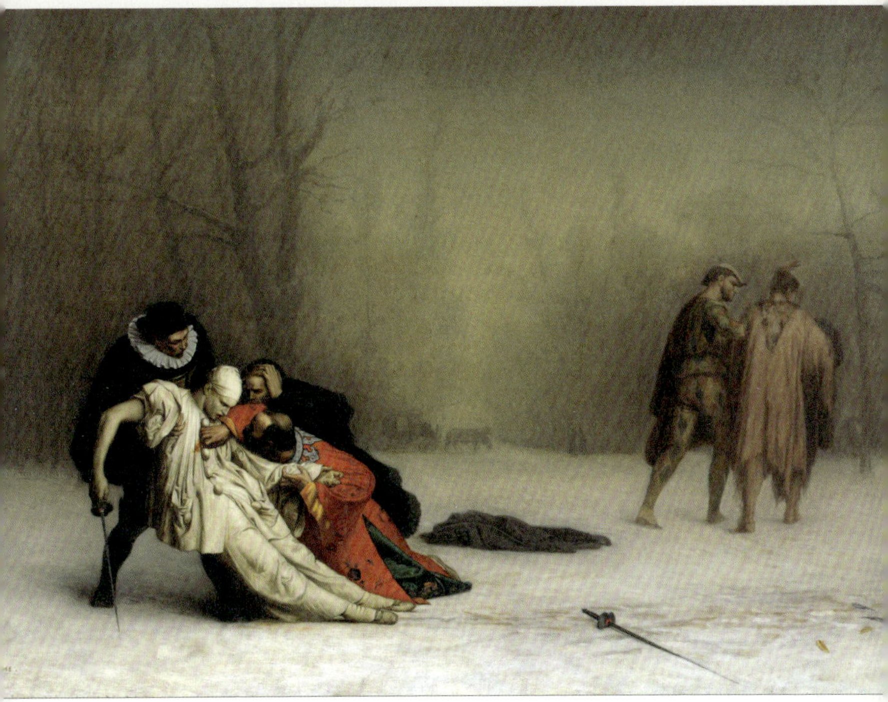

Now there is one thing I can tell you: you will enjoy certain pleasures you would not fathom now. When you still had your mother you often thought of the days when you would have her no longer. Now you will often think of days past when you had her. When you are used to this horrible thing that they will forever be cast into the past, then you will gently feel her revive, returning to take her place, her entire place, beside you. At the present time, this is not yet possible. Let yourself be inert, wait till the incomprehensible power...that has broken you restores you a little, I say a little, for henceforth you will always keep something broken about you. Tell yourself this, too, for it is a kind of pleasure to know that you will never love less, that you will never be consoled, that you will constantly remember more and more.

——**Marcel Proust** 1871-1922 : *Letter to Georges de Lauris*

生死，人生歷程的始末

現在我能告訴你：你將來必然會享受到一些你現在還無法領會的樂趣。當你的母親還健在時，你常想著沒有她的日子。而現在，你會開始不時想起她還在世的過往。當你習慣「他們將永遠被拋進過往」這件可怕的事情之後，你會漸漸感受到她的復活，回歸她的位置，她所有的位置，就在你身旁。目前這還是件不可能的事。你就先讓自己一蹶不振吧，直到那曾摧毀你的神祕力量將你復原一些，因為日後你將永遠保有你被摧毀的某些部份。你就這麼告訴自己：你將不再愛得更少、你再也無法得到安慰、你會不斷回憶起越來越多往事——因為知道這些，本身就是種樂趣。

——普魯斯特，致一位剛喪母的友人書信

We have only a little time to please the living. But all eternity to love the dead.

——**Sophocles** c. 296-405 BC : *Antigone*

生死，人生歷程的始末

我們只有少許時間能取悅生者，卻有完整永恆能敬愛死者。

—— 古希臘劇作家索福克勒斯《安蒂岡妮》

From the standpoint of daily life, however, there is one thing we do know: that we are here for the sake of each other—above all for those upon whose smile and well-being our own happiness depends, and also for the countless unknown souls with whose fate we are connected by a bond of sympathy. Many times a day I realize how much my own outer and inner life is built upon the labors of my fellow men, both living and dead, and how earnestly I must exert myself in order to give in return as much as I have received.

——**Albert Einstein** 1879-1955 : *Living Philosophies*

從日常生活的觀點看來，有件事無論如何都是確定的：你我都是為了彼此而存在於此，尤其是為了我們的喜悅寄託在他們的微笑與幸福之上的那些人。同時也是為了那些經由同理心與我們命運相連的陌生靈魂。一天當中，我總會數度理解到，自己的外在與內在生活是如何建立在同儕的勞動上，不論其生死，而我又該如何克盡己力，以付出同等回報。

—— 愛因斯坦《生活哲學》

Perfection of character is this: to live each day as if it were your last, without frenzy, without apathy, without pretence.

——**Marcus Aurelius** 121-180 : *Meditations*

人格的完備在於此：將每天都活得像是你的最後一天，不衝動、不冷漠、不造作。

——奧里略《沉思錄》

To look life in the face, always, to look life in the face, and to know it for what it is...at last, to love it for what it is, and then, to put it away...

——**Michael Cunningham** 1952- : *The Hours*

生死，人生歷程的始末

直面生命，總是直面生命，並且如其所是地認識生命⋯⋯最後，如其所是地愛生命，然後再將它拋去⋯⋯

——麥可・康寧漢《時時刻刻》

生死，人生歷程的始末

ILLUSTRATIONS

Jacket: *Selbstporträt mit Fiedelndem Tod* (1872), Arnold Böcklin
Cover: *La Canestra di frutta* (1598), Caravaggio

I.

1. *Ritratto di Don Manuel Osorio Manrique de Zuniga* (1787-88), detail, Francisco de Goya
2. *Disparates* (1808-12), Francisco de Goya
3. *Wild Geese in Flight* (1897), Winslow Homer
4. *Still Life with the Hunting Trophy* (1660s), Melchior d'Hondecoeter
5. *Island of the Dead* (1883), Arnold Böcklin
6. *Anguish* (1876-80), August Friedrich Albrecht Schenck

II.

1. *Figures of Death Rob a Village of Its Children* (1890), Stefano della Bella
2. *Mortalia Facta Peribunt*, Anonyme
3. *Allegory of Vanity* (1632-36), Antonio de Pereda
4. *L'Inhumation précipitée* (1854), Antoine Wiertz
5. *Égalité devant la mort* (1848), William Adolphe Bouguereau

III.

1. *Sleep and His Half-Brother Death* (1874), John William Waterhouse
2. *Cloister Cemetery in the Snow* (1817-19), Caspar David Friedrich
3. *Dance of Death* (1660), Franciszek Lekszycki
4. *Memento mori* (17th Century), Wilhem Alzenbach
5. *Vanitas* (1671), Philippe de Champaigne

IV.

1. *The Conversion of the Duke of Gandia* (1884), José Moreno Carbonero
2. *The Triumph of Death* (1562), Pieter Bruegel the Elder
3. *Saint Francis Receiving the Stigma* (1585-90), El Greco
4. *The Burial of the Count of Orgaz* (1588), El Greco
5. *The Death of Socrates* (1787), Jacques Louis David

V.

1. *Dog Guarding Dead Game* (1753), Jean Baptiste Oudry
2. *The Angel of Death* (1881), Evelyn De Morgan
3. *Vanitas* (1663), Evert Collier
4. *The Ambassadors* (1533), Hans Holbein the Younger
5. *Les disciples Pierre et Jean courant au sépulcre le matin de la Résurrection* (1898), Eugène Burnand
6. *San Girolamo in Meditazione* (1605), Caravaggio

生死，人生難解的結未

7. *Suites d'un bal masqué* (1857), Jean-Léon Gérôme
8. *Self-Portrait with Love and Death* (1875), Hans Thoma

生死,人生難題的永恆探索……等人

譯者／王姿婷

總編輯／富察
主編／林家任
執行編輯／林子揚
行銷企劃／蔡慧華、廖珮杏
編輯顧問／洪源鴻

設計／井十二設計研究室

社長／郭重興
發行人兼出版總監／曾大福
出版發行／八旗文化・遠足文化事業股份有限公司
地址／新北市新店區民權路108-2號9樓
電話／02.2218.1417
傳真／02.8667.1065
客服專線／0800.221.029
信箱／gusa0601@gmail.com

法律顧問／華洋法律事務所．蘇文生律師
印刷／通南彩色印刷股份有限公司

出版日期／2017年10月／初版一刷
定價／新台幣310元

1.生死觀 2.電影特寫
197
10601628

ISBN 978-986-95418-3-1 (平裝)
304面；13×21公分
八旗文化，遠足文化，2017.10
初版，新北市
房慧真著；王姿婷譯
生死,人生難題的永恆探索

Complex Chinese translation © 2017 by Gusa Press, a Division of Walkers Cultural Enterprises Ltd.
ALL RIGHTS RESERVED
中文翻譯版權所有・翻印必究